S0-ACO-036

"Bernard Evans has written a valuable book for every Catholic voter (and others as well). He makes it very clear that voting, a moral obligation, is an expression of one's faith. I think chapter 5, 'Promoting a Pro-life Agenda,' is especially helpful in deciding on a candidate when no one candidate's position on various life-issues satisfies all our moral concerns. He stresses, and rightly so, that voting on a single issue is not voting responsibly. *Vote Catholic?* teaches us to vote the Gospel!"

—Bishop Victor H. Balke
Diocese of Crookston, Minnesota

"In an age of single-issue politics, the marriage of extremist religious and political ideologies, and competing values and agendas, Bernard Evans offers some down-to-earth common theological sense about what should guide Christians when they vote. Firmly rooted in Catholic social teaching, issues like promoting the common good, the dignity and value of all human life, and the 'preferential option for the poor,' are central concerns in this context. While written specifically as a guide for Catholics, Christians of various denominations will find this extremely helpful as well. The summaries and study guides at the end of each short chapter make this an extremely useful text for adult education in parishes and schools. Here is a book that needs to be read!"

—Maxwell E. Johnson
Department of Theology
University of Notre Dame

Vote Catholic?
Beyond the Political Din

Bernard F. Evans

LITURGICAL PRESS
Collegeville, Minnesota

www.litpress.org

Nihil Obstate: Rev. Robert C. Harren, J.C.L., *Censor deputatus.*
Imprimatur: Most Rev. John F. Kinney, J.C.D., D.D., Bishop
of St. Cloud, December 21, 2007.

Cover design by Ann Blattner.

Excerpts from documents of the Second Vatican Council
are from *Vatican Council II: The Basic Sixteen Documents*, by
Austin Flannery, OP © 1996 (Costello Publishing Company,
Inc.). Used with permission.

Scripture texts in this work are taken from the *New Revised
Standard Version Bible* © 1989, Division of Christian Education of the National Council of the Churches of Christ in
the United States of America. Used by permission. All
rights reserved.

© 2008 by Order of Saint Benedict, Collegeville, Minnesota.
All rights reserved. No part of this book may be reproduced
in any form, by print, microfilm, microfiche, mechanical
recording, photocopying, translation, or by any other
means, known or yet unknown, for any purpose except
brief quotations in reviews, without the previous written
permission of Liturgical Press, Saint John's Abbey, P.O. Box
7500, Collegeville, Minnesota 56321-7500. Printed in the
United States of America.

1   2   3   4   5   6   7   8   9

Library of Congress Cataloging-in-Publication Data

Evans, Bernard F.
    Vote Catholic? : beyond the political din / Bernard F.
Evans.
        p. cm.
    ISBN 978-0-8146-2946-8
    1. Christianity and politics—Catholic Church.
2. Catholic Church—Doctrines.   3. Catholics—Political
activity.   I. Title.

    BX1793.E93 2008
    261.7—dc22   2007041523

To Bob Carvajal,
whose passion for justice and politics
gave lasting shape to the
Catholic Campaign for Human Development.

Contents

Introduction   ix

Chapter 1
Connecting Faith and Justice   1

Chapter 2
Promoting the Common Good   14

Chapter 3
Opting for the Poor   27

Chapter 4
Protecting Human Life and Dignity   42

Chapter 5
Promoting a Pro-life Agenda   55

Chapter 6
Roles   70

Chapter 7
Beyond Elections   83

Conclusion   96

Introduction

In the Gospel of Luke we read that Jesus began proclaiming the kingdom of God by announcing good news to the poor, release to captives, sight to the blind, and freedom to the oppressed (Luke 4:18-19). It was a message familiar to his listeners—a reading from the prophet Isaiah. The prophets of the Old Testament frequently reminded the people that their relationship with God required them to give special care to the poor and vulnerable among them—the widows, orphans, and strangers.

Today our response to Jesus' preaching must be marked by repentance, conversion, and change of life. Like the people hearing Jesus in the synagogue in Nazareth and like those to whom the prophets spoke, this conversion is tested by our response to persons whose needs are great.

The Catholic Church teaches that we should reach out to the poor with charity and justice, through direct services and through changing systems and structures so that everyone may do well. One way to promote such change is by electing leaders committed to building a more just society.

In recent years there has been much discussion—and confusion—about how Catholics should vote. Some of this is caused by individuals and organizations seeking to advance particular agendas. Some of it is the result of honest uncertainty among Catholic voters, especially regarding candidates who may not agree with official church teachings on various issues, abortion being the most obvious among them.

This book attempts to sort out and evaluate some of the more strident claims about how Catholics should vote. The sources for this task are the universal social teachings of the church as well as pastoral statements on voting that have come from the Catholic bishops here in the United States (the most recent of which, Forming Consciences for Faithful Citizenship, was released in the late stages of this book's publication, allowing time and space for only brief reference). It is the conviction of this writer that our church's teachings invite us to vote with particular attention to three areas:

1. protecting human life and the dignity of all persons,
2. promoting those living conditions that allow everyone to do well,
3. giving particular attention to the "widows, orphans, and strangers" of our day.

To vote in this way flows out of our gratitude for Jesus' announcement that the kingdom of God is at hand. It is not easy to vote in this way, for it calls us to examine our values and change our lives. However, the payoff for this approach to casting our ballots is very large and goes beyond our personal benefits. To vote in this way may help the poor to hear the good news, the captives to gain release, the blind to recover sight, and the oppressed to experience freedom. Indeed, our vote does matter.

Chapter 1

Connecting Faith and Justice

Religion and politics do mix!

Most of us grew up hearing some version of the opposite claim. We learned that politics and religion make bad bed partners. Religion should stay out of politics and politics should have as little as possible to do with religion. Persons engaged in politics would do well to check their religion at the door. And if the rest of us must talk about politics, let us not inflame an already volatile subject by dousing it with religious viewpoints.

It's difficult to know the origins of this popular attitude regarding the separation of religion and politics. Some people fear the tragic consequences that usually follow a blending of political power and religious fanaticism—a historical reality that continues into the present time. For others, this preferred separation might be a way to ensure harmony when the family gathers for a peaceful Thanksgiving dinner. Whatever its origins, the customary nod to the separation of religion and politics continues in this day, even after the walls of separation have been cracked, breached, and, in some instances, removed altogether.

Religion, Church, Faith, and Politics

Not only are religion and politics actually mixing all the time, they *should* mix! Still, there is much confusion around this topic. The separation of church and state can mean keeping religion and politics apart. More broadly it can suggest not letting faith or religion influence political choices. This first chapter seeks to clarify these claims and to make the case that religion and politics do (and should) in fact mix.

Religion and Politics

We begin by recognizing that politics and religion often come together in unhealthy ways. Political leaders justify policies as enjoying the approval of God. The war in Iraq is discussed using the language of "a righteous nation" at battle against "the forces of evil." Candidates seeking election to public office align themselves with particular congregations, even taking the Sunday pulpit. Others brashly proclaim that God told them to run for office, suggesting in yet another way that God takes sides.

For their part religious groups try to influence public policy as well as specific elections. Inviting a favorite candidate to preach at Sunday worship is one example. Another is buying a full-page newspaper ad to "educate" Catholics about the so-called five nonnegotiable issues to use in assessing candidates. This particular blending of religion and politics typically focuses upon a very limited number of issues and tends to distort the church's teachings on how Catholics should vote.

Yet another way we miss the mark on the relationship between politics and religion is to dismiss the connection entirely. Many persons, including some politicians, are uncomfortable with the language of religion and faith. Others have not thought through the connection between religion or faith and politics. Still others believe that their religion and faith commitments should remain separate from positions they take on public policies. Several years ago a diocesan social action director in Minnesota was talking with a congressional staff person about the Catholic bishops' position on a particular piece of legislation. The conversation faded when the staff person pointed out that "the congressman tries not to let his faith convictions influence his political decisions."

Religion and Civil Society

Most Americans are familiar with the notion of separation of church and state, even if we have wildly different understandings of its meaning. This notion is grounded in the First Amendment to the Constitution of the United States which reads: "Congress shall make no law respecting an establishment of religion, or prohibiting the free exercise thereof." That's it! That's all we find in the Constitution and Bill of Rights (the first ten amendments) on this question of how church and state or religion and politics should relate.

This amendment argues two points. The first is that the state shall not recognize any one religion above the others, and the second is that the state shall not interfere with the free exercise or practice of religion. Though a clear separation between church (any church or religion) and the state, this still leaves a lot of room for religion or a church to interact with the offices and agencies of the state. Indeed it leaves much room for the church to influence politics and the formation of public policies. The church may even engage in lobbying for specific pieces of legislation—within certain guidelines and restrictions. What religion, understood here as institutional church, may not do is engage in partisan political activity such as supporting a particular candidate during an election campaign. Apart from that the church, like any other nongovernment organization, enjoys a wide range of options to pursue in influencing the state or engaging in political activity. The critical issue is not *whether* religion may interact with the state and its political entities. The issue is *how* religion chooses to exercise this right to help shape society.

> *The critical issue is not whether religion may interact with the state and its political entities. The issue is how religion chooses to exercise this right to help shape society.*

Through its core ministries of worship, evangelizing, and service, each church enjoys extensive opportunities to shape the values of its members. Beyond these core activities of all churches, religion also may influence more directly how society formulates public policy related to specific topics. One example is the recent effort by many churches against gay marriages and in support of constitutional amendments defining marriage. Here is an example of religion shaping society's values in a general way through preaching and teaching its members. At the same time through its political activity religion here seeks to influence public policy regarding marriage.

Role of Faith

However we look at the role of religion in politics, we must not overlook the centrality of faith in the life of the individual Christian. From a Catholic perspective faith must guide every area of our lives. If faith has something to do with receiving and responding to the good news of the Gospel, that response must be reflected throughout our lives and in every moment of our lives, not just our Sunday attendance at Mass.

Both the prophets of the Old Testament (Isa 58:6-9) and Jesus Christ in the New Testament (Matt 25:31-46) condemned this scandal of separating faith from daily lives. The Second Vatican Council warned that "one of the gravest errors of our time is the dichotomy between the faith which many profess and their day-to-day conduct" (Church in the Modern World, 43). There should be complete separation neither between religion and politics, nor between an individual's faith and political activity. That faith should guide us in our relationships, families, schools, workplaces, social settings—and political activity.

At the same time we need to develop a healthy integration of faith and life. That is not easy, and that is where we may find many different viewpoints even within the Catholic Church. Still, that should not surprise us since the institutional church itself has struggled over the years to articulate the proper relationship between the faith of church members and their political commitments.

How Do They Relate?

Today the United States bishops encourage Catholics to be actively involved in politics. Every four years, during the presidential election campaign, the bishops write a pastoral letter calling on Catholics to participate in the electoral process and to do so from a faith perspective. Their message: let your religion, your faith, shape your political choices. This has not always been the position of the church's leadership.

Accepting Political Involvement

Prior to the writing of the modern Catholic social encyclicals the laity in the church were not encouraged to take part in politics. Through the eighteenth and much of the nineteenth centuries Rome cautioned against the laity being involved in democratic self-governance. The image of the uneducated masses choosing their own political leaders did not sit well with the church's hierarchical leadership. A change in that attitude came with the first Catholic social encyclical, On the Condition of Labor (*Rerum Novarum*), in 1891. Pope Leo XIII cautiously accepted the right of workers to unionize and to bargain collectively. In doing so he acknowledged the right of ordinary people to participate in political decisions that affected their lives. Seventy years later Pope John XXIII noted that taking leadership roles in places of employment would prepare workers to help govern society (Christianity and Social Progress, 96–97).

Expecting Political Involvement

It was in the Second Vatican Council that these early seeds of faith-driven political involvement came to fruition. The Pastoral Constitution on the Church in the Modern World stated that every nation should allow all its citizens to participate in governance, to shape society's institutions and to choose leaders (75). Pope Paul VI was particularly blunt in calling the laity to take an active part in the political affairs of their nation. It is up to the laity, he wrote in 1971, "without waiting passively for orders and directives, to take the initiative freely and to infuse a Christian spirit into the mentality, customs, laws and structures of the community in which they live" (A Call to Action, 48). Five years later the U.S. Catholic bishops began their presidential-year practice of encouraging Catholics to engage in the political process and to do so under the guidance of their faith.

Church Mission

The question of mixing politics and religion relates especially to the behavior of individual Christians and the extent to which their faith guides political choices. But the politics and religion question also pertains to the church as an institution within society. How we address that question depends largely upon how we understand the mission of the church.

No Political Mission

With his first encyclical, Pope Benedict XVI disappointed some Catholics by stating that the political task of building a just social order "cannot be the Church's immediate responsibility" (God is Love, 28). Although he was granting this position an emphasis not seen in recent decades, the core of his statement was not new to Catholic social teaching. The 1971 World Synod of

Bishops taught that it is not the church's responsibility "to offer concrete solutions in the social, economic, and political spheres for justice in the world" (Justice in the World, 37). The Second Vatican Council stated in even clearer terms that Christ "did not bequeath to the church a mission in the political, economic, or social order" (Church in the Modern World, 42).

In spite of these statements we find the United States Catholic bishops writing in 2007 that the church as an institution is involved in the political process (Forming Consciences for Faithful Citizenship, 58). How are we to reconcile these seemingly contradictory positions on the mission of the church? The answer is found most readily in what all statements refer to as the "religious mission" of the church. Out of this religious mission comes a need for the church to be involved in the affairs of the world (Church in the Modern World, 42).

As noted earlier, it is wrong to think that religion is only about worshiping and following a set of moral laws. Religion is more than a ticket to heaven. The daily affairs in which all of us are involved cannot be divorced from our life of faith, from our religious calling. Nor can the mission of the church—a religious mission—be separated from social, economic, and political happenings in the world.

A Religious Mission

This political dimension of the church's religious mission arises out of its primary responsibility to preach the Gospel of Jesus Christ. The Gospel calls all of us to conversion from sin, to acceptance of God's love, and to universal love of our brothers and sisters throughout the world. That love carries a demand for justice in the world, a demand to remove any barriers that prevent the realization of this universal love.

Injustices of any kind contradict the fundamental message of the Gospel that the church is called to preach. They lead to enmity, hatred, and divisions, and they happen in the concrete, practical realities of life—in the poverty wages paid to laborers, in the denial of healthcare to uninsured citizens. The church's denunciation of these injustices must be equally clear and practical or its preaching of this Gospel will not be heard.

The church engages in the political realm because that is where practical changes can be made in unjust living conditions that contradict the Gospel message of universal love.

Jesus calls all of us to conversion: "Repent, and believe in the good news" (Mark 1:14). This is a call not only to turn away from something but to turn toward something. Our response to this call is to accept God's love and direct our lives toward God. For this each of us is responsible (On the Development of Peoples, 15). But we also recognize that a person's living conditions can either promote or hinder one's development and response to God's call. Hunger or homelessness can limit a person's ability to respond to God. These conditions—and other forms of injustice—leave many people with "no chance whatever of exercising personal initiative and responsibility" (Church in the Modern World, 63). Without that freedom and responsibility it is difficult for any of us to respond to the church's preaching that we are loved, redeemed, and called to communion with God.

The church engages in the political realm because that is where practical changes can be made in unjust living conditions that contradict the Gospel message of universal love. The church accepts this political dimension of its religious mission because she recognizes that the ordinary, daily aspects of life influence how we live out our vocations and respond to God's redeeming love (Catechism of the Catholic Church, 2420).

Connecting This Life and the Next

Political involvement—by individual Christians and by the institutional church—is grounded in a Catholic sense of the mission of the church. It also reflects our understanding of the connection between this life and that which awaits us.

A New Human Family

Catholic theology refers to the life to come as a "new earth," a realm of justice, love, and peace, a kingdom in which human nature and human efforts will be cleansed and perfected (Justice in the World, 75). One of the most beautiful images of the connection between the present imperfect human life and that which is to come is found in Pastoral Constitution on the Church in the Modern World:

> Far from diminishing our concern to develop this earth, the expectation of a new earth should spur us on, for it is here that the body of a new human family

grows, foreshadowing in some way the age which is to come. (39)

Gone is any suggestion that belief in an afterlife should counsel patient acceptance of poverty and injustice in this life. Belief in a life after death is the reason for seeking to improve life here on earth, because there is a connection between the present and future lives. The human community is the body of a new human family and in this family we already see the life that is to come. What a hopeful thought! We already are a reflection of that perfected human family. In spite of all our shortcomings, sinful failures, and inability to live justly and peacefully, our very imperfect but redeemed lives are able to "[foreshadow] in some way the age which is to come."

Change and the Need for Politics

To "develop this earth," to improve living conditions especially for the poor and marginalized, to change unjust systems and structures is the work of social justice, and it is part of the church's mission. A Catholic understanding of social justice implies two values. First is that each person should contribute to the well-being of the entire community. Most of us do this by caring for those close to us, through our work, our volunteering, and our willingness to pay taxes.

Social justice also implies that society must make it possible for everyone to contribute. If persons or groups live in extreme poverty, or are homeless, or without food, or worry about medical needs for their uninsured children—for such persons it can be difficult to care for themselves much less to contribute to the larger community. That is why social justice also means we are willing to change whatever prevents people from living a full, dignified life. In Catholic thinking, social justice always means systemic, structural change.

This need for societal change, especially in economic matters, often requires political action. Pope John Paul II reminded us that a nation's economic system must be guided by society and by the state (On the Hundredth Anniversary of *Rerum Novarum*, 35). This is the way to ensure the satisfaction of all society's basic needs—like health care or reasonable immigration policies. We know that in these and so many other matters "the ultimate decision rests with political power" (A Call to Action, 46).

Participating in Politics

Social justice is the way to build a healthy society, and politics is one of the primary arenas in which this building takes place. Christians, then, need to be active in both social justice and politics. This right to participation is also a responsibility, a duty to take part at some level in the political process where so many decisions are made regarding the common good. At a minimum each of us can participate in politics by electing to public offices those persons most likely to guide the state or nation in ways that promote the good of all.

Our Christian faith should influence our political choices and commitments, just as that faith should guide us in all other areas of our lives. The church's religious mission includes a direct concern about how the social, economic, and political aspects of our lives influence our moral growth. In this manner religion touches politics—on both the individual and institutional church level. In this sense we may say that religion and politics both do and should mix. The issue is not whether but how. From a Catholic perspective there are three especially important criteria for guiding us in living out this sometimes-tense relationship between religion and politics. We focus upon these in the next three chapters.

Discussion Points:

- To say that religion and politics do mix is to recognize that our religion—and our faith—should influence our political choices. It also acknowledges that organized religion—the church—has a legitimate role in shaping the social, economic, and political structures of society.

- Catholics are called to be politically active and to allow their faith convictions to shape their political commitments.

- The church's mission is religious, but that religious mission includes a concern for how the social, economic, and political aspects of our lives influence our moral growth.

- Because this life already is a foreshadowing of the life to come, our faith urges us to do all we can to improve living conditions for everyone, and especially to challenge any injustices.

- In Catholic teaching, social justice tells us that each person should contribute to the good of the larger community and that society must make that contribution possible.

Chapter 2

Promoting the Common Good

Gubernatorial candidate pledges no new taxes!

This newspaper headline during a Minnesota political campaign said a lot about one of the candidates for governor. It also told us that a sizable percentage of the voting public has a negative attitude toward taxes. That's hardly news. Worth noting is how political candidates today boldly play to this individualistic and antigovernment attitude within the public. This sentiment contrasts with traditional American values like community-mindedness, civic engagement, and a willingness to help others in need.

The matter of taxes is complex and there can be many legitimate reasons for citizens choosing not to support a particular tax hike. A problem with no-new-tax pledges, however, is that they fail to consider community needs or the ideals and values that define who we are as a state or nation. They also tempt us to overlook the truth that our well-being as individuals depends upon the health and success of the larger community. This also reflects Catholic teaching on the common good—one of three criteria for living out the relationship between religion and politics, for guiding us in voting and in all of our political commitments. That is the focus of this chapter.

Common Good

The language of the common good is as present in Catholic social thought as it is absent from our culture. These are not words you hear in ordinary conversations and certainly not in major speeches by political leaders. However, it should be a primary concern of Catholics when discerning the worthiness of a candidate or position.

So That All May Do Well

The meaning behind these words is often reflected in public discussions about societal needs like funding for education or ensuring universal access to health care. A debate on these topics is a debate about the common good. It is a discussion about changes needed in society so that everyone can enjoy a better life. The national debate about immigration too often is sidetracked into rantings about losing our identity, proclaiming an official national language, and keeping out terrorists. The immigration debate should be a discussion about how our nation can accept immigrants in a manner that is welcoming of new arrivals while responsible to our national economic, political, and security interests. All of these are discussions about ever-changing practical needs that lead us to build a society in which everyone can do well.

That is the core meaning behind the phrase, "promoting the common good." This phrase provides the connecting fiber to basic principles and themes in Catholic social teaching—rights and responsibilities, option for the poor, solidarity. The common good refers to all those living conditions (social, economic, cultural, political) that permit all persons in society to achieve their own fulfillment (Church in the Modern World, 74). To promote the common good means to help bring about those conditions, and they cover every aspect of our lives—jobs and income, medical needs, educational opportunities, adequate housing. They include resources upon which we depend as a community—transportation systems, the environment, different forms of financial and social security, parks, and recreational amenities. Promoting the common good includes responding to persons with particular needs—the unborn and the elderly, the poor and the homeless, the sick and the imprisoned. We do this because we know that we as a society cannot do well unless everyone in society is doing well.

> *The immigration debate should be a discussion about how our nation can accept immigrants in a manner that is welcoming of new arrivals while responsible to our national economic, political, and security interests.*

Local and Global

Promoting the common good means helping to bring about those living conditions that encourage all of us to develop ourselves, to realize our sacred dignity, and to become the persons God calls us to be. The Christian call to universal love and solidarity directs us to promote the common good on the local, national, and global level. This can happen most easily in the communities where we live. There we find opportunities to assist others, to volunteer, or to help shape public policies and programs affecting life in our communities. But we also can stay informed of news events and support national policies that promote a better quality of life for everyone beyond our local and state boundaries. Finally, our call to promote the common good invites us to pay attention to the global community with its challenges and needs. Here we might try to appreciate how our nation's policies and actions promote or hinder the common good in other nations through trade policies, foreign aid, or military actions. We might seek to understand, for example, the complaint from other countries that government price supports of U.S. agricultural products hurt farmers in less-developed countries.

Our Social Nature

We need to promote the common good—locally, nationally, globally—because of who we are. We are social beings who live, grow, and develop in contact with other people. We need one another. We depend on others to teach, guide, and help us throughout our lives. It is in interaction with others that we come to know ourselves and our place in this world. Our family members, friends, and other social contacts map out the direction of our lives and the paths we must follow to "achieve our own fulfillment."

Parents often tell young children how their friends can influence their behavior. It is equally important to recognize how the broader social environment of our lives affects our development through our entire lifetime.

The quality of an educational system may determine how well students do later in life. Welfare policies that penalize recipients for meager earnings do not teach good work habits. A minimum wage that allows thousands of full-time workers to remain in poverty doesn't do much to help struggling families achieve their own fulfillment.

As social beings we need healthy families and good friends to guide us through life. We also need economic, political, and social structures that support our development and our interaction with others. If we don't have that, our focus will be more on survival than on the social and spiritual growth that leads us to be concerned about the betterment of others. We are social beings, dependent upon one another and our social environment so that we may "achieve our own fulfillment" and in turn promote the common good.

Making a Single People

Promoting the common good means doing whatever each of us can to help build a society that allows all persons to do well. We do this because of how we see the human person: social and dependent upon relationships to guide our journey. We do this also for fundamentally religious reasons.

People in Covenant

The biblical story of the Hebrews is that of a people and their relationship with God. It is especially a story of God's love and care for this people, a story of what God expected from this people. Central to this relationship was God's expectation that the people of Israel would look out for one another. The U.S. Catholic bishops emphasized this point in their 1986 document Economic Justice for All: "Biblical faith in general, and prophetic faith especially, insist that fidelity to the covenant joins obedience to God with reverence and concern for the neighbor" (37).

This concern for the neighbor included particular attention to those who were poor and marginalized—the widows, the orphans, and the strangers. In the prophetic literature, the justice of the community was measured by how it cared for the powerless:

> Thus says the Lord: Act with justice and righteousness, and deliver from the hand of the oppressor anyone who has been robbed. And do no wrong or violence to the alien, the orphan, and the widow, or shed innocent blood in this place. (Jer 22:3)

In gratitude for God's saving acts on their behalf when God rescued them from slavery in Egypt, the Israelites were to treat the poor and the stranger as God had treated them. This was a demand of Israel's covenantal relationship. Caring for the neighbor in need was one of the expectations that flowed from their relationship with God. It defined the justice of the people.

Going to God Together

This biblical emphasis upon the connectedness of all people continues to shape contemporary views on church and salvation. The Second Vatican Council emphasized the communal nature of our stance before God:

> Just as God did not create people to live as individuals
> but to come together in the formation of social unity,
> so he "willed to make women and men holy and to
> save them, not as individuals without any bond be-
> tween them, but rather to make them into a people
> who might acknowledge him and serve him in holi-
> ness." (Church in the Modern World, 32)

This is an affirmation of our social character and more.
Not only are we social beings who need one another to
live reasonably well in this life, but we also go to God
as a people. Our journey to God, our response to the
saving acts of Christ is shaped by our life together.

> *. . . the individual's needs are best met in the context of addressing everyone's needs.*

It is natural then that we live
with a sensitive awareness of
the lives of others. Certainly we
need to take care of ourselves
and those who depend upon
us, especially within our fami-
lies. Our own needs must be met or we will not be in a
position to help anyone. But we are called also to do
what we can to help others realize their dignity. We do
this most commonly through our family life as well as
our work, volunteering, charitable contributions, and
through the taxes we pay.

God's desire to save us by making us into a single
people must become for us a desire to help shape that
people, a grateful willingness to let our own lives be
formed and guided by this larger project. That is a view
that asks us to consider our needs, and especially our
wants, in relation to the larger society. This view chal-

lenges us to see that what we own or what we seek to possess or the lifestyle we follow has an effect—for good or bad—on the larger community.

This is another way of saying that the individual's needs are best met in the context of addressing everyone's needs. Obviously we as individuals cannot reach out to every person in the community, but we are members of a society that can address such needs. Our task is to promote those policies and programs of society— public and private—that support everyone's journey. Working for the common good in this way is how we address our nation's needs. This is not being purely altruistic because we know that when everyone does well, we will do well.

A Demanding Ethic

Promoting the common good is a demanding moral precept. Working for the betterment of everyone goes counter to some of our cultural values, such as independence, competitiveness, and individualism. This is not the drumbeat of too many political campaigns. At the same time our best human intuitions tell us that happiness and good fortune cannot come to us at the expense or even neglect of others. Americans' generous response to persons in need or to communities suffering from a flood or tornado reflects that intuition. Our faith draws us further along this path to see that our support of others in need should be an ongoing attitude and way of life.

It is a demanding ethic, and we don't always measure up to its expectations. Indeed, our tendency often is to hold back, to "take care of our own" (family members, local community, national needs). These can be legitimate interests. They also can be rationalizations preventing us from striving to make our contribution to the common good. However short we may fall from its realization, we need this ideal to draw us further than we ordinarily wish to go.

Role of Government

One specific challenge in promoting the common good is to recognize the legitimate role of government in this task. There are many views on government at any level—from "the best government is the least government" to "let the government take care of all social needs."

In Catholic social teaching we find the principle of subsidiarity, suggesting that larger units of government should not do what smaller, more local entities can do for themselves. This teaching also argues that the primary responsibility of government is to promote and safeguard the common good—to promote "those conditions of social life which enable individuals, families, and organizations to achieve complete and effective fulfillment" (The Church in the Modern World, 74). To do this, to carry out its responsibility of furthering the common good, government must enjoy the support of the governed. This points to a responsibility that rests on all of us. It also provides us with a way of promoting the common good that we cannot possibly do on our own.

Needs and Resources

Elections offer an opportune time to promote the common good. The political campaigns leading up to elections create a moment for asking what our society needs in order for everyone to do well. For all persons to realize their fulfillment, what changes are needed? What resources are called for, and who might provide the necessary leadership? If government has a role in promoting the common good, then election campaigns are times for public debate about that function of government and especially about the needs of society at that moment.

Elections and Society's Needs

It should be the starting point of every candidate's election campaign to ask: what does our society need? Individuals should not seek public office solely to advance their own political careers, nor to champion a single cause such as ending abortion or cutting taxes. No single issue can adequately represent the comprehensive needs of society. Further, this broader assessment of social needs should constitute both the candidates' and the voters' point of entry into election campaigns. We begin by asking: what does society need?

Our second critical question should address how those needs can best be met. Who are the candidates most suited to addressing society's major needs? What segments of society need to be mobilized to meet these needs? What is my role? What about the private sector? The nonprofit, volunteer realm? What is the place of government in confronting these current challenges facing society? What level of government—local, state, federal—is best suited to help resolve particular problems or provide needed services?

Candidates and the Common Good

In the midst of election campaigns, we then ask which candidates have the vision and strategies for addressing society's needs. If we are called to contribute to the common good—to help create a social environment that allows everyone to do well—then our assessment of candidates for public office must go beyond identifying which candidate's policies benefit us personally. That is a legitimate factor in determining how to vote, but not the only one. A richer and far nobler stance is to ask which candidate's policies and positions are best for society.

One of the most difficult challenges facing candidates for public office is dealing with the issue of taxes. For many voters and advocacy groups, taxes have become the single issue by which to evaluate candidates. In response to strong antitax sentiments, political candidates often begin their campaigns with a promise or pledge or some other form of assurance that they will not raise taxes. Sadly, this position too often is taken before any public discussion of society's needs. This is backwards! Besides appealing to our most individualistic instincts, this approach fails to consider what is needed to promote the common good in this nation (or state or local community) at this time.

In meeting our responsibility to promote the common good every one of us—candidates and voters—must be willing to provide government with resources needed to carry out its functions. This does not mean we have to support every proposed tax increase. It does mean, however, that we are open to the possibility of providing new revenues if we judge this will meet a genuine need.

In his 1967 encyclical, Pope Paul VI reminded us that the duty of solidarity calls us to a spirit of generosity in meeting human needs both at home and throughout the world. He called upon each of us to examine our conscience and ask if we are prepared to support out of our own pocket "works and undertakings organized in favor of the most destitute?" Are we "ready to pay higher taxes so that the public authorities can intensify their efforts in favor of development? (On the Development of Peoples, 47). The Holy Father recognized the role of government in promoting the common good. He also recognized the twofold responsibility of citizens to provide their government with the necessary resources to do its job, and to elect to public office candidates willing to use that office to promote the common good. To do that means giving particular attention to persons and groups with greater needs. This leads us to the second criterion for guiding our choices in the political realm, which we will consider in the next chapter.

Discussion Points:

- The common good refers to all those living conditions (social, economic, cultural, political) that allow everyone in society to realize their own growth and fulfillment.

- We are social by nature, and Catholic theology points out that God desires to save us, not merely as individuals, but by making us into a single people.

- Our own happiness and well-being depends upon the well-being of others—our families and friends as well as the communities and societies in which we live.

- Government, at all levels, has a primary responsibility of promoting the common good.

- Elections, and the campaigns leading up to them, are an especially good time to consider and promote the common good.

Chapter 3

Opting for the Poor

Poorest families use 50 percent of their wages for rent.

A 2007 report from the Department of Housing and Urban Development reveals that six million of America's poorest families use most of their monthly earnings for housing. These six million families received no federal rent assistance. Housing experts point out that for the past several years our nation has been shifting money away from domestic assistance programs to pay for tax cuts and the wars in Iraq and Afghanistan. Government programs simply don't have enough money to help those families most in need of housing assistance.

This report on our nation's failure to provide needed housing assistance to poor families is more than a story about housing issues. It brings to light the larger question: How serious are we about addressing poverty? In reference to the previous chapter, where do the needs of the poor fit in our efforts to promote the common good?

Few among us would argue that we should not help people in need, especially if we claim to be followers of

Jesus Christ. That position does not fit well with the one who went around healing the sick, feeding the hungry, dining with social outcasts, and proclaiming good news to the poor. We may disagree on how best to help persons in need, particularly those who are economically poor. Different strategies, however, do not suggest disagreement on the fundamental claim that as individuals and as a society we should reach out to help persons living in poverty.

How does our recognition of this moral responsibility relate to the political process? More specifically, what does it have to do with voting? Catholic teaching always has stressed the need for individual citizens and for government policies and programs to assist the poor. Today, with greater democratic processes in place, how government responds in this area often is determined by how the voting public expresses its wishes through the electoral process. How we vote can be an important way for us to respond to the needs of the poor. This chapter focuses on the "option for the poor," the second criterion in Catholic social teaching to guide our political choices.

Responding to Persons in Need

Being willing to help people is a fairly fundamental expectation of Christian morality—of living the Christian life. As disciples of Christ it is a given that we are to love our neighbor and that this love must be shown in practical actions. Speaking and acting on behalf of the neighbor in need is an important way for the church to preach the Gospel of Jesus Christ (Justice in the World, introduction).

A Biblical Emphasis

The Acts of the Apostles tells us that the ideal early Christian community shared all things in common so that "there was not a needy person among them" (Acts 4:34). Much has been written about the meaning of this early Christian sharing of possessions. This communal ownership of goods apparently did not continue long into the history of the church, but it clearly was an effort to help persons with economic needs. Clearer still, this holding of all things in common sought to ensure that within the Christian community there would be no one with economic needs, there would be no one in poverty.

In 1 Corinthians, St. Paul admonishes Christians to tend to one another's needs before celebrating the Eucharist. He noted that it was no longer one common meal that the followers of Jesus shared in conjunction with the Eucharist. Rather, the more affluent among them feasted while the poorer members of this same faith community stood by hungry. Such a division within the community—both then and now—contradicts what is celebrated in the Eucharist. Christ's life, death, and resurrection makes everyone equal members of this church, this Body of Christ.

In the parable of the Last Judgment in Matthew 25, Jesus made it clear that our response to persons in need is a nonnegotiable expectation for entry into the kingdom of God:

> Come, you that are blessed by my Father, inherit the kingdom prepared for you from the foundation of the world; for I was hungry and you gave me food, I was thirsty and you gave me something to drink, I was a

stranger and you welcomed me, I was naked and you
gave me clothing, I was sick and you took care of me,
I was in prison and you visited me . . . Truly I tell you,
just as you did it to one of the least of these who are
members of my family, you did it to me. (Matt
25:34-40)

The followers of Christ distinguish themselves by love
for one another and by caring especially for those who
are weak and poor and vulnerable. This is an expectation that flows from our relationship with Christ. It also
is a characteristic of our life together in the Body of
Christ, the church.

A Church Response

Within the Catholic Church we find many structured
opportunities for responding to persons in need. These
avenues allow the church and individual members to
join with others to address the immediate needs of the
poor as well as the more systemic factors that contribute
to poverty. Three such examples are especially worth
noting.

Catholic Charities is most familiar to lay parishioners.
Operating in most dioceses since the early 1900s, Catholic Charities offers numerous programs to help people—
such as housing, food assistance, financial counseling,
and refugee resettlement. Catholic Charities also engages
in justice advocacy for public policies that address the
causes of poverty. Since 1971 the Catholic Campaign for
Human Development has been making grants to combat
poverty through local, self-help, social change projects
throughout the United States. These projects aim to

change whatever factors cause people to live in poverty. They aim directly at systemic, institutional change. A third example of structured Catholic opportunities to respond to peoples' needs is Catholic Relief Services (CRS). This is an international effort by the Catholic Church in the United States to respond to the needs of the poor and marginalized throughout the world. CRS offers both direct services and development projects designed to help communities move out of poverty.

These three examples of organized efforts within the Catholic Church model how each of us might respond to people whose income leaves them struggling to make ends meet. They also represent practical opportunities for us to contribute financially and to volunteer our time and gifts to assist others. Most important, Catholic Charities, the Catholic Campaign for Human Development, and Catholic Relief Services bear witness to a central Christian belief that has endured over the centuries. That is, to be a follower of Jesus Christ, to be a Christian, means that we use our gifts, talents, and resources to improve the lives of others, especially those who lack what is needed to live a dignified life.

Measurement of a Just Society

Helping people to live a dignified life and making it possible for others to have what they need for such a life is part of what it means for each of us to live a Christian moral life. We believe that we as church are not fully the Body of Christ if we are not engaged in charity and justice actions on behalf of the marginalized. We also believe that the state itself has a responsibility in this area.

Distribution of Goods

It is a function of government, a responsibility of the state, to ensure that all members of society have the opportunity to participate fully in society. This is the surest way of making available to all the goods and services required for a dignified life. This is another way of expressing government's primary purpose of promoting the common good—helping to create those "conditions of social life which enable individuals, families, and organizations to achieve complete and effective fulfillment" (The Church in the Modern World, 74). Persons and groups who exist on the margins of society must be a particular focus of such efforts.

This is the measurement of a just society—its efforts to include all persons, but especially the poor, in its progress. In 1961 Pope John XXIII observed that a country's economic prosperity should be measured, not in the total of goods and wealth possessed, but in the "distribution of goods according to norms of justice" (Christianity and Social Progress, 74). This necessarily means that persons with greater needs must have access to society's goods and services.

Correct Disparities

Reflecting on this in 1986 the U.S. Catholic bishops insisted that "the poor have the single most urgent economic claim on the conscience of the nation" (Economic Justice for All, 86). If their needs are not addressed in ways that go beyond charity, a nation cannot claim that it is properly and adequately tending to the common good.

Such an effort involves more than providing direct services to the needy. It especially means making whatever changes are needed in our society to ensure that everyone—including and especially the economically poor—are able to improve their lives and contribute to the common good. These state or government efforts may relate to economic changes, such as increasing the minimum wage or in other ways ensuring a truly living wage for all workers. It may require government initiatives in health care reform to ensure that the current forty-seven million Americans without health insurance are able to receive necessary medical services. The state may need to change the way communities finance education to provide greater access to equal education regardless of race or residence.

> *"the poor have the single most urgent economic claim on the conscience of the nation" (Economic Justice for All, 86). If their needs are not addressed in ways that go beyond charity, a nation cannot claim that it is properly and adequately tending to the common good.*

For a society to be healthy and to prosper it must pay attention to persons existing on the fringes. This is not only a moral requirement. It is also good public policy. Social scientists at times see a correlation between rising poverty and increased crime rates. They also remind us that it is economically advantageous for a society to help low-income persons move out of poverty and into the ranks of workers able to care for themselves and pay taxes. Yet today in the United States there is a growing disparity between persons of great affluence and power on the one hand, and those at or near the poverty threshold on the other. One percent of Americans hold 19 percent of this nation's income, the largest share since 1929. The poorest 20 percent of Americans hold 3.4 percent of the income. This is not the mark of a society committed to justice for all. Pope John Paul II wrote that a society that refuses to deal with these issues, such as the need for adequate employment and income for all workers, "cannot be justified from an ethical point of view, nor can that society attain social peace" (On the Hundredth Anniversary of *Rerum Novarum*, 43).

Preferential Option for the Poor

In the previous chapter we noted that one criterion for choosing candidates for public office is to ask which candidates have the best vision and strategies for addressing society's needs by promoting the common good. This chapter makes the case that responding to the needs of the poor and vulnerable is a second criterion or characteristic of a Catholic approach to voting. That is to say, we should consider those candidates who demonstrate a willingness to have government exercise its responsibility to look out for those who have the greatest needs. This does not mean government alone must help the poor. That task belongs to all of us. It does suggest, however, that in promoting the common good the government pays special attention to the most vulnerable among us, to those who enjoy little or no influence in the political process. In Catholic social teaching we call this the preferential option for the poor.

Biblical Grounding

Although "option for the poor" language is of relatively recent origin, its meaning is rooted in the ancient texts of the Judeo-Christian tradition. The Old Testament speaks about widows, orphans, and strangers. These were the people of that time and place who were particularly vulnerable. They symbolized the poor of that culture.

The prophets of the Old Testament often chastised the people of Israel because they neglected the poor. Worse, the rich and powerful were accused of abusing the poor, as in Isaiah: "What do you mean by crushing my people, by grinding the face of the poor? Says the Lord God of Hosts" (Isa 3:15). The prophets frequently pointed to this neglect of the poor as a sign that Israel was not living up to the expectations of its covenantal relationship with God, that the people of Israel were not living justly.

To be in right relationship with God required, among other things, that the people be in right relationship with one another. That expectation included the call to show particular care to the poor and the marginalized, for the people of Israel were once enslaved and marginalized in Egypt. Just as their God led them to freedom and new life through the Exodus, so now they were expected to show that same care for the poor in their society.

This message is also found in the teaching and actions of Jesus of Nazareth. In the Gospel of Mark, Jesus begins his public ministry by reading from the Isaian text that highlights the good things that are dawning for those most in need: the blind see, the lame walk, the poor have the Gospel preached to them. To the chagrin of his own disciples, Jesus spends an embarrassing amount of time with social outcasts like tax collectors, prostitutes, and Gentiles. And Matthew injects into the Last Judgment a criterion about serving the least of my sisters and brothers (Matt 25:40).

Early Christian Writings

Ambrose of Milan, writing in the fourth century, presented what would become the rationale for the Christian's obligation to share with those in need: the universal purpose of the goods of creation. Everything in creation is given to meet the needs of everyone. Using the biblical story of Ahab and Naboth, Ambrose points out that the greedy of the world unjustly seek and hold what is not theirs. Thus, Ambrose warns the avaricious that even in acts of charity: "You are not making a gift of your possessions to the poor person. You are handing over to him what is his" (Naboth 12:53). Even more broadly does John Chrysostom apply this obligation of the more affluent to assist the poor: "The rich are in possession of the goods of the poor, even if they have acquired them honestly or inherited them legally" (On Lazarus, Homily 11).

Catholic Social Teaching

Modern Catholic social teaching after the Second Vatican Council draws directly from this early Christian emphasis on the universal purpose of the goods of creation. In a 1967 encyclical Paul VI uses the above quote from St. Ambrose and then adds the following emphasis:

That is, private property does not constitute for anyone an absolute and unconditional right. No one is
justified in keeping for his exclusive use what he does
not need when others lack necessities. (Development
of Peoples, 23)

These teachings—from early Christian writers and from
papal social encyclicals—remind us that in a world of
limited resources but growing needs, those of us blessed
with abundance must be willing to share with those
who are not. The goods of the earth are intended to meet
the needs of everyone.

A final development of this theme is the introduction
and use of "option for the poor" language, which first
appeared in a 1971 apostolic letter from Pope Paul VI:

In teaching us charity, the Gospel instructs us in the
preferential respect due to the poor and the special
attention they have in society: the more fortunate
should renounce some of their rights so as to place
their goods more generously at the service of others.
(A Call to Action, 23)

This moves beyond the simple issue of sharing with those
in need. It argues that we also must take steps—renounce
some of our rights—so that we are in an even better position to share. The matter is no longer just about possessions but about whatever else we can do to demonstrate
this "preferential respect due to the poor."

Option for the Poor and Social Justice

Combined with a Catholic understanding of social
justice, this preferential respect for the poor becomes a

preferential option for the poor. It means that when faced with various options related to social change we choose that course of action most likely to benefit the poor. It means that we are willing to support those changes in public policies, laws, programs, economic and social systems that are of greatest benefit to those with the greatest need. It means making this choice—this option—even when we do not see how these changes may benefit us personally.

Political and Strategic Implications

Structural changes in society usually do not happen without strong guidance and advocacy. The state or government has a role to play in helping to bring about these changes—changes that will benefit those most in need, changes that are at the heart of promoting the common good. In a representative democracy like the United States, we the citizens have an equally important place in directing the government to make these changes.

Electing Candidates

Through the electoral process we determine who will serve in those governmental positions that shape our nation's laws, financial decisions, programs, and public policies. Through our votes we can determine whether we as a nation are willing to make the changes required for everyone to be able to live a life of dignity. The electoral process is a way for us to exercise our preferential option for the poor.

Among the many decisions we make at the polls is that of deciding whether we will help to elect candidates who seem willing to work on behalf of the needs and rights of the marginalized. This is not an easy task. It can be difficult to know who those candidates are. The voices of the poor and vulnerable are not usually heard during election campaigns. Their needs are rarely mentioned during political debates. It is difficult because political campaigns tend to reflect current values and preferences of the voting public. These values too often are marked by overt ten-

> *It means that when faced with various options related to social change we choose that course of action most likely to benefit the poor.*

dencies toward seeking our personal advantage and satisfying our own needs. Further, the current political climate makes it even more difficult by focusing anger and mistrust on issues like immigration, exploiting fears about national security, and responding more readily to well-financed special interest groups. It may be hard to identify those working for the marginalized, yet the option for the poor calls us to support those changes— and candidates who will work for those changes—that are of greatest benefit to those most in need.

Range of Issues

Perhaps the most effective way to recognize candidates with a commitment to help the marginalized is to focus upon issues that most affect the poor. These include health care, housing, living wage, education, public assistance, and immigration. Candidates willing to engage these issues are likely to recognize the challenges we need to face if we are to promote the common good.

Politicians who recognize this understand that the common good cannot be realized unless it is realized for everyone. Each of us does well when all of us do well.

There are other issues of concern to all of us that relate directly to the well-being of the marginalized. Violence in our society is an example. Whether in the form of assaults, abortion, or capital punishment—violence in any of these forms takes its heaviest toll upon persons with less means. The destruction of the environment is felt most by those least able to cope with such realities as toxic waste sites in their communities or a factory allowed to operate on the margins of environmental responsibility. Our nation's international trade agreements, foreign assistance, and military actions affect people everywhere, and these policies are decided by the people we elect to the legislature and White House.

On all these issues, the persons we choose to send to Congress or the White House can determine whether our nation's policies and programs will help or harm those less well off. The preferential option for the poor calls us to elect persons who demonstrate a willingness to consider these, "the least of my sisters and brothers," wherever they live, to elect officials willing to make the interests of the marginalized a priority in their legislative agenda. This teaching also calls us to vote for candidates committed to protecting the life and dignity of all people, the focus of the next chapter.

Discussion Points:

- The option for the poor is grounded in a biblical call to assist our neighbor in need.

- The early Christian writings developed the principle of the universal purpose of the goods of creation.

- Social justice and the preferential respect for the poor lead to the preferential option for the poor.

- Working to improve life for the poor and the vulnerable is an essential aspect of promoting the common good.

- One way to make the option for the poor is to elect candidates who as government leaders will respond to the needs of the marginalized.

Chapter 4

Protecting Human Life and Dignity

Bishop to candidate: No communion in my diocese!

During the 2004 presidential election campaign a few Catholic bishops made headlines by declaring that candidate John Kerry was not welcome to receive communion in their dioceses. Kerry, a Catholic, held positions on abortion that disagreed with official church teaching. The media, of course, paid little attention to the fact that the U.S. Catholic bishops as a body had taken a rather different position on how we should examine candidates and issues. Still, this short-lived controversy illustrated that there is confusion—even among a few bishops—on the place of abortion and other human life issues in an election campaign.

In previous chapters we noted that promoting the common good is one of the criteria for determining who should receive our vote. That is, we should consider which candidate has the best understanding of what society needs at this time and is most committed to meeting those needs. Within this promotion of the common good we recognized a second voting consideration: opting for the poor. Creating social conditions in which everyone can do well must include and even give priority to persons and groups that are most disadvantaged.

There is a third voting consideration at the heart of Catholic thinking about society and the human person: protecting human life and dignity. In Catholic social thought there is no principle or theme more foundational. If we are not able to recognize the dignity of every human being and the sacredness of all human life, then we will struggle to appreciate the importance of all other issues, whether social, economic, cultural, or political. All of them relate in varying degrees—but directly—to the human person.

If we are not able to recognize the dignity of every human being and the sacredness of all human life, then we will struggle to appreciate the importance of all other issues, whether social, economic, cultural, or political.

The notion of human dignity enriches our way of looking at each person. It also provides insight on how we should organize and structure society. Protecting human life and dignity leads us to examine whether society's laws, programs, systems and policies enhance or threaten the life and dignity of all people. In Catholic thought we often carry out this critique along two main question lines: what in our society represents a direct attack against human life; and, how might society more effectively enhance the life and dignity of each person. Both of these questions have implications for how we vote.

Resisting All Attacks against Human Life

To honor the dignity of every person and the sacredness of each human life means that we are ready to defend every life. We make a fundamental presumption in favor of all life and against any action that would end a human life. That is our starting point—that life is a gift granted by God and only God may withdraw that gift and allow a life to end. Each human life must be allowed to run its course from conception to natural death. Our society today contains a number of practices, policies, and laws that contradict this belief. Each of these should enter into our decisions about voting.

Abortion and Embryonic Stem Cell Research

Two topics that immediately come to mind in this discussion are abortion and the use of embryonic stem cells in medical research. The Catholic Church's opposition to abortion is well known, grounded as it is on the claim that human life begins at conception. For that reason an abortion at any stage of a pregnancy is morally unacceptable.

The issue of stem cell research is far more complex and challenging to understand. The use of adult stem cells presents no problem to Catholic moral theology, obtained as they are from bone marrow and other body tissues. Embryonic stem cells, however, are taken from fetuses which are then discarded. In Catholic teaching this is the moral equivalent of abortion and the benefits realized from the use of embryonic stem cells do not justify the means employed to get them.

The complexities of this issue—evident in the ongoing scientific and technological developments—can be difficult for most of us to understand. What we can appreciate is that embryonic stem cell research, in so far as it involves the destruction of human embryos, is morally unacceptable.

Euthanasia and Assisted Suicide

Two other forms of direct attacks against human life are euthanasia and assisted suicide. Euthanasia often involves an effort to end the life of a person who is seriously ill or dying. It goes beyond the morally acceptable practice of choosing not to receive or administer extraordinary medical procedures that are disproportionate to the expected outcome and that may cause a financial burden to family members. Assisted suicide might be carried out for good motives such as a desire to end the suffering of a loved one. To directly and intentionally end a human life, even when the action is accompanied by good intentions, is morally unacceptable. It represents as well a failure to recognize the dignity and sacredness of that person's life.

Death Penalty

The death penalty represents yet another direct attack upon human life. Throughout most of its history the church has shown little opposition to capital punishment, believing in the state's right to defend its citizens against extremely violent criminals. While that responsibility of the state continues, church teaching no longer accepts that capital punishment is a necessary means to this end. This shift in church teaching is clear in the writings of Pope John Paul II, who stated that punishment of offenders should not include execution except where this is the only way to defend society. "Today, however, as a result of steady improvements in the organization of the penal system, such cases are rare if not practically nonexistent" (Gospel of Life, 56). To be clear, the state retains the right to use the death penalty when it judges such action necessary to protect citizens. Catholic teaching makes the point, however, that the duty to defend citizens can be realized today without executing convicted criminals. In the United States, especially, there no longer is a need to exercise the theoretical right to use this lethal action.

Terrorism and War

Two additional examples of attacks against human life are acts of terrorism and war. Here we need to be clear that whatever motive leads to either of these activities, the actions themselves represent direct and violent attacks against humans and sometimes the rest of God's creation as well. The acts of terrorists may rise out of long-standing suffering and injustices, and they may be accompanied by good motives. But cause and motivation can never justify actions that are fundamentally wrong. Acts of violence intended to harm or kill innocent human beings are always immoral.

War of any kind and for any purpose involves the destruction of human life. There are, of course, important differences between the moral quality of some wars on the one hand, and terrorist actions on the other. A nation has the right to defend itself. That defense may involve the use of arms after all efforts at peaceful means have been exhausted. We should note, however, that this Catholic position regarding legitimate warfare begins with a presumption in favor of peace. The Catholic bishops made this point in their 1983 pastoral statement, The Challenge of Peace: God's Promise and Our Response:

> The Church's teaching on war and peace establishes a strong presumption against war which is binding on all; it then examines when this presumption may be overridden. (70)

The traditional just war criteria offer a means for determining when it is morally acceptable to set aside the presumption against war, in other words, when it is legitimate for a nation to go to war.

Today there is much discussion about whether these moral criteria developed so many centuries ago—and under such a different experience of war—can provide the moral guidance needed in today's world. However we answer that question, three points merit emphasis. First, we must remember always that these criteria seek to prevent war, not justify an already made decision to go to war. Second, we should recognize also that the just war criteria always will present us with a temptation to seek justification for our violent actions, rather than to work faithfully for justice and peace so that the conditions that breed hatred, violence, and war may be kept in check. Third, however justified we may feel about our nation entering a war, we must remember that war represents a direct attack against life. Both combatants and civilian noncombatants become victims of our inability or unwillingness to avoid armed conflict and to prevent over time the conditions that lead us to this tragic moment. However skillfully we may articulate the moral arguments to support a particular war, to these victims the conflict comes as an attack against their desire and right to continue living.

Enhancing Life and Human Dignity

Besides direct attacks, we can recognize other ways in which human life is diminished and the dignity of the human person threatened. In the United States today too many peoples' needs go unmet, too many people for whom basic human dignity is threatened daily. As individuals and as a society we have many opportunities to address peoples' unmet needs. Four examples are especially worth noting because they point to serious needs but also hold promise of positive action. For that reason, how we decide to vote, especially in state and national elections, should consider candidates' positions on health care, living wage, immigration, and the environment.

Health Care

Making sure that everyone in this society has access to basic health care is one practical way of enhancing the life and dignity of all. Catholic social teaching counts medical care among the basic human rights (Peace on Earth, 11). Every person should have ready access to needed medical services, and every society should seek the best way to ensure this right.

Today in the United States more than forty-seven million Americans do not have health insurance. Many unhappy personal and social consequences flow from this. Too many individuals postpone needed medical treatments because they can't afford them. Many delay treatment of a minor condition until it reaches a critical state, resulting in an even costlier medical procedure. Others turn to emergency wards where they are assured medical attention even if they cannot pay. Our nation's failure to ensure every citizen access to needed medical treatment means that we have a less healthy population. It also means that we are spending an excessive amount of our resources in providing health care in a manner that is neither effective nor efficient.

Fixing the health care problem is not impossible. Already several states have initiated a variety of approaches to providing health insurance to state residents. Some efforts focus on children, some on low-income residents. Others require employers to provide basic health coverage, or citizens to purchase a minimum amount of insurance. Many nations provide universal coverage, Canada being one example. Though we may have quite different assessments of these efforts, we should be able to agree that ensuring access to needed health care service in this country must be a priority. How that is done, and whether it is done on the state or federal level, is what we need to debate. One place where all of us can enter that debate is the election campaigns.

Living Wage

A living wage should be more than a dream and a hope for working people. This is the issue that launched the writing of Catholic social encyclicals in 1891 (On the Condition of Labor). The definition of a just wage has developed over the past hundred years. What has not changed is the insistence that a just wage—a living wage—allows workers to meet their needs and live in dignity.

In the United States today millions of workers earn less than a living wage. We may have different views on what constitutes a living wage, but surely we can agree that this wage will keep a worker above poverty. Yet today more than a million Americans work full time at wages that leave them below the federal poverty line. Our response to this problem typically focuses upon raising the minimum wage. In 2007 the United States Congress raised the minimum wage for the first time in ten years. Today a person working at this newly increased minimum remains at least three thousand dollars below the poverty line.

As with health care, we may not agree on how best to ensure that workers receive a wage sufficient for themselves and their dependents. Surely we can agree that for any workers, but especially those with families, poverty wages are not the way to enhance human life and dignity. This is an issue of great concern to our society and one deserving serious discussion and debate during political campaigns.

Immigration

A third area in which political campaigns can contribute to the enhancement of human life and dignity is that of immigration. This topic is complex and can be difficult to understand. Out of it rises such questions as why people leave their homelands, what responsibilities a host nation has regarding immigrants, and how to treat both legally documented immigrants and those who have come without proper documentation. Many of these questions become the basis for current legislative proposals to deal with immigration issues. Absent from some of these proposals is any attempt to consider pertinent moral questions.

Catholic social teaching presents many of these moral considerations, including the recognition that the goods of the earth belong to all people. A joint pastoral letter from the Catholic bishops of Mexico and the United States in 2003 reminded us of everyone's right to emigrate in search of a livelihood: "When persons cannot find employment in their country of origin to support themselves and their families, they have a right to find work elsewhere in order to survive" (Strangers No Longer, 35). Nations have the right to control their borders, but this is not an absolute right. Implicit in the right to immigrate is the claim to basic necessities required to live a dignified life including livable wages, health care, housing, and education. All immigrants—regardless of their legal status—have a legitimate claim to these minimum conditions for respectable living.

In the United States there may be as many as eleven million undocumented immigrants. Most of them are contributing to the well-being of our society by working and paying taxes. Many of them earn money not only for themselves but to send back to family members in their homeland. It is hardly an exaggeration to say that the food industry in this country, including agriculture, is dependent upon the labor of undocumented immigrants. A similar dependency exists in other sectors of our economy such as the hotel and construction industries. It appears, then, that this nation's economy relies upon and benefits from an immigrant labor force while our laws make it impossible for these laborers to enter the United States legally.

During the past few years we have seen numerous legislative proposals put forward to address immigration issues. As with the topics already discussed, this one allows for different perspectives and different approaches. From a Catholic moral perspective, a starting point is to recognize that this is not simply about stopping illegal immigrants from entering our country. Our nation needs to reform its immigration laws with particular attention to the needs of immigrants, to the labor needs of employers, and to the security concerns of the United States.

> *Our nation needs to reform its immigration laws with particular attention to the needs of immigrants, to the labor needs of employers, and to the security concerns of the United States.*

This is a topic that belongs in the discussions and debates surrounding candidates for public office. Because of its importance in our society today, and because our church has such a long commitment to the well-being of immigrants, this is a topic that should influence how we vote.

Environment

A fourth topic that ought to shape our thinking about public policy and voting is the environment. Catholic teaching about creation is clear on how we should look upon the natural world in which we live and upon which we depend for our existence: it is a gift from God. Drawing upon the creation stories (Gen 1 and 2) and other biblical texts, this teaching recognizes that all the world and everything in it belongs to God (Ps 24). In their 1991 pastoral letter on the environment, the U.S. Catholic bishops reflect on the truth that everything in creation depends upon God:

> For the very plants and animals, mountains and oceans, which in their loveliness and sublimity lift our minds to God, by their fragility and perishing likewise cry out, "We have not made ourselves." (Renewing the Earth, p. 6)

If God is the creator of all, and if God has given this creation to support our lives, then we must care for it as stewards watching over what belongs to someone else. This applies to anything we own and use. It applies as well to the goods of creation we share in common with other peoples and other creatures.

Today there are signs that we have failed to care for God's creation. Perhaps none stand out as clearly as global warming. For years we have debated whether this is a real problem and whether it is caused by human behavior. While there remain many debatable aspects to this issue, few today would deny that the answer to both questions is "yes."

Our response to global warming—or to any environmental issue—should be on two levels at least. One is to examine how our personal lifestyles contribute to the problem, and to ask what we are willing to change. The other is to engage larger structural changes by joining with others to remedy the problem. One way to do this is through the electoral process.

This and all the issues related to human life and dignity carry within them the hope of resolution. As we consider how to vote, we would do well to bring that hope forward and ask which candidates offer the best chance of moving ahead on these issues. As we focus on candidates, we also need to ask which of these issues is most pressing today and which office or level of government is best suited to respond. This is material for the next chapter.

Discussion Points:

- Three criteria especially should guide us in deciding how we will vote: 1) promoting the common good, 2) opting for the poor, and 3) protecting human life and dignity.

- Along with abortion, euthanasia, and assisted suicide, other actions represent direct attacks against human life. Among these are the death penalty, terrorism, and war.

- Catholic teaching on peace and war calls us to work faithfully for justice and peace so that the conditions that breed hatred, violence, and war may be kept in check.

- In Catholic social teaching every person has a right to needed medical care.

- The foundation of Catholic teaching on immigration is the early Christian principle that the goods of creation are given to meet the needs of everyone.

Chapter 5

Promoting a Pro-life Agenda

I voted 100 percent pro-life!

Nothing fuels a debate regarding "pro-life" as much as a national election. During political campaigns, Catholic organizations remind us that we must vote pro-life. Candidates buy ads in diocesan newspapers proclaiming their opposition to abortion and touting their pro-life voting record in the House or Senate. In the heat of an election campaign, little effort is made to define pro-life or to ask what issues constitute a pro-life stance.

How are Catholics to decide which candidates deserve their votes? Clearly there is no perfect candidate, no one person who satisfies all expectations voters might have. What happens when a candidate advocates for the poor but also supports abortion legislation? In this less-than-perfect political environment some Catholic groups offer certain "nonnegotiable issues" as automatic guides for choosing candidates. This is a highly dubious approach and one that misrepresents official Catholic teaching (e.g., U.S. Catholic bishops) on how we should vote.

Previous chapters presented fairly general criteria to assist us in voting—promoting the common good, opting for the poor, and protecting human life and dignity. This chapter explores how we might use these three criteria in promoting a truly pro-life agenda through our voting. We begin by defining what we mean by "pro-life" and recognizing the variety of issues that constitute a pro-life stance.

Pro-life: From Conception to Natural Death

For some Catholics the term "pro-life" means being antiabortion. Period! This is an unfortunate diminishment of the full, rich meaning of pro-life as held by most Catholics and by the teachers of the church.

In the latter view, to be pro-life means to protect, respect, and enhance human life from the moment a person is conceived until that person leaves this world through natural death. The United States Catholic bishops summarize this teaching in their 2003 statement, Faithful Citizenship:

> Human life is a gift from God, sacred and inviolable. Because every human person is created in the image and likeness of God, we have a duty to defend human life from conception until natural death and in every condition. (17)

This definition of what it means to be pro-life appears in a pastoral statement on how Catholics should go about their responsibility of voting. The bishops do not elaborate. Rather, they expect Catholics to know that being pro-life means protecting the life and dignity of all people throughout their entire lives.

Resisting Attacks Against Life

Being pro-life certainly means we stand against any direct attacks against human life, such as abortion, euthanasia, and assisted suicide. But a consistent Catholic pro-life stance also calls for opposition to capital punishment and war.

In a 1999 homily in St. Louis, Pope John Paul II reminded us that the death penalty "is both cruel and unnecessary," a point that led the bishops to say that resistance to the death penalty "is part of our pro-life commitment" (Faithful Citizenship, 19). It is in this discussion as well that the bishops locate their comments on war. While acknowledging that military force may sometimes be used as a last resort "to defend against aggression," they express "serious moral concerns and questions about preemptive or preventive use of force."

Promoting the Life and Dignity of All Persons

To be pro-life means more than resisting direct attacks against human life. It also means promoting the conditions that enable all persons to live in dignity and realize their own fulfillment. It means promoting the common good with particular concern for the poor and the vulnerable.

Conditions that promote dignity and life can vary widely throughout the world and even within our own country. This can be complex and difficult to understand especially regarding causes and best solutions. What is not complicated is the simple recognition that a person's sacred dignity is not fully protected when she has no place to sleep or cannot afford needed medical help for her children.

In the Catholic world being pro-life includes promoting a quality of life at every stage, at every age. It is never enough simply to defend a person's right to be born. To be pro-life means striving to see that all persons have the basic necessities for living a dignified life. Thus, being pro-life necessarily leads us to look at the social and economic issues of our day, and to ask whether they can be improved for all persons.

To focus solely on abortion, or the death penalty, or health care, or immigration, or any other one issue may be a quick and easy way to choose among candidates. . . . This may be a convenient way to proceed, but it is not responsible.

Recognizing Political Realities

Promoting a pro-life agenda today invites us to see that there are many issues demanding our attention. It means that in deciding how to vote we ask which candidates are most likely to protect life and promote the dignity and quality of human life for everyone.

No Single Issue

A pro-life agenda guides us to make the best choice we can when none of the candidates "measure up" to Catholic teaching about the dignity of all human life. This agenda never limits our attention to a single issue, no matter how serious that issue.

To focus solely on abortion, or the death penalty, or health care, or immigration, or any other one issue may be a quick and easy way to choose among candidates. Any set of "nonnegotiable issues" can serve as an automatic check-off approach to evaluating candidates for public office. This may be a convenient way to proceed, but it is not responsible.

Even when we name a topic as the most important issue, it still is not the only one to consider during an election campaign. We might be most concerned about the right of a child to be born—but that is just the beginning of this person's life outside the womb. Between birth and natural death there are countless factors that determine how well or how poorly this person will move through life. We must direct our attention to at least some of these conditions of living when assessing the qualities of political candidates.

Diversity of Perspectives

In sorting through the qualities of various candidates we should consider as well the diverse character of the voting public. Many voters do not share the same religious or faith basis that guides our commitment to certain issues. These voters—neighbors and fellow citizens—may not see as important the topics we judge to be critical. This does not mean we should back away from what we consider to be the most important matters of the day. Indeed, we should expect our faith to lead us to positions that might conflict with popular, cultural standards.

At the same time, we need to recognize that among voters there are many different and legitimate viewpoints. Other citizens are evaluating candidates' positions on many other issues. We need to be part of that public discussion regarding the entire range of issues, because all of them impact the realization of the common good. Yet it is difficult for us to participate in this broad discussion if we focus only on one or two issues.

Political election campaigns in their best form are about the challenges and opportunities of our day. They are about asking how in this society at this time we can most effectively promote the common good. How can we create those social conditions that allow everyone to do well?

To answer these questions we must explore where candidates stand on such topics as the reform of immigration, as well as abortion and the death penalty. We must examine their positions on a range of issues affecting the health of families in our society—like living wages for workers, or the provision of affordable child care. In short, it means that we recognize the important topics of our day and ask which candidates are best suited to lead us as a society in addressing them.

Staying Informed

To promote a pro-life agenda in this manner requires that we keep ourselves informed of what is happening in our nation and throughout the world. This is not an easy task in a culture where regular news programs increasingly take the form of news-lite entertainment. Staying abreast of current news and events is an important step toward informed, responsible voting. Without this information we risk casting our votes on the basis of political ads aimed more at the destruction of opponents than at the discussion of serious issues. Without this information we are all the more likely to vote by single issues. That approach may be easier and it may even feel right. It does nothing, however, to promote a full pro-life agenda through the ballot box.

Supporting Multiple Approaches

Promoting a pro-life agenda requires a variety of approaches. Any serious effort to protect the life of the unborn or to ensure health care services to everyone or to stop the executions on death row will involve a variety of strategies such as education, organizing, advocacy, and prayer. A commitment to protect human life and defend human rights must recognize that no one activity can bring about the desired end. This is particularly so with pro-life issues that can be controversial and open to varied interpretations.

Legislation: One Approach

Most Americans would agree that all Americans should have access to needed health care services—a basic human right in Catholic social teaching. Beyond that, however, there is little agreement on how these services should be made available to all. For that reason anyone committed to seeing medical services become a guaranteed right must work on many fronts: educating the public about the need and possible solutions, advocating on behalf of the forty-seven million Americans currently without health insurance, and organizing in political forums to advance needed legislation. Another strategy could be attempting to elect candidates to public office who support your views on health care. It is important to realize, however, that no single one of these strategies—including the last one—will by itself bring about the desired goal.

The same can be said of many other pro-life issues: abortion, capital punishment, obtaining a living wage for workers, and affordable housing. Too often we settle for single-strategy approaches, especially where there is a question of defending human life against direct attacks. Frequently that approach is narrowly political—electing to office someone we believe will pass a law or support a constitutional amendment. When that strategy succeeds—the election of an antiabortion candidate, for example—many activists end their involvement in the matter. They simplistically believe that electing this candidate ends their responsibility on the issue. Sadly we often don't notice that these candidates whom we supported because of their "pro-life" promises have done little or nothing to advance this agenda—a reminder that we need to work on pro-life issues using several different strategies.

Looking to Other Approaches

Legislation is one way to address an issue, but it is not the only way and sometimes not the best way. Electing a legislator to carry the necessary bill may be helpful to the effort, but it never represents more than a part of the effort. Education, lobbying, advocacy, and organizing all have their place in protecting human life and promoting the sacred dignity of every person. Depending on the issue, time, and place, any one of these strategies may carry more importance than electing the right candidate.

In looking to other approaches it is important to know the most current information about the issue. Social science research, for example, might lead a death penalty opponent to recognize that morally grounded appeals may not be the most effective way to end this practice. More successful might be an approach that seeks to educate legislators on the higher financial costs of capital punishment as well as other problems inherent in the system. In January 2003, for example, Illinois Republican Governor George Ryan commuted all 156 death penalty sentences in that state. Governor Ryan had not necessarily changed his mind about the morality of capital punishment, but he judged the system unable to prevent sentencing people to death on wrongful convictions.

Similar considerations might help us discover new strategies for limiting the number of abortions in the United States. Not every abortion occurs because the mother doesn't want the child. Some women, especially if they live in poverty, make that choice because they don't have the financial means to raise the child. A strategy to decrease abortions might be to work for increased social services to support both mother and child during the early childhood development years.

Prioritizing Issues

As we try to decide how to vote for political candidates, most of us engage in some level of issue prioritizing. It is difficult not to. We tend to identify more strongly with some issues than with others.

Some of us regard abortion as the premier issue against which to evaluate candidates. Others may focus on where candidates come down on providing universal health care. Still others might identify capital punishment as the most important pro-life issue. This prioritizing of issues in an election campaign presents both dangers as well as possibilities.

Dangers

Prioritizing issues risks making a single issue the only one we consider during a campaign. The problem here is not that we identify one topic as important to ourselves and our society. As already noted, we all do that to some extent. Rather, the danger is in perceiving this topic as the most important one always and for everyone. The tendency here is to assert not only that each candidate should hold my position on this issue but that other voters should be where I am as well.

Another danger in prioritizing issues in this manner is that it often renders us unable to recognize or respond to other needs facing society. When the highly prioritized single issue becomes the standard by which to judge candidates, it is difficult to give due consideration to other topics. The logic of this kind of prioritizing suggests that all time and resources should be directed to this priority problem. Only after its resolution should we work on other topics. By contrast, Catholic social teaching calls on us to promote the common good by addressing all of society's needs.

Further, absolutizing one or a few issues can blind us to practical realities. To use abortion as an example, we might ask if it makes sense to judge candidates by where they stand on abortion if the office to which they aspire has no chance at all of dealing with this issue. Or, if it is clear that in the foreseeable future neither the state legislature nor Congress will take up this issue, is it even responsible to evaluate candidates by where they stand on abortion? Certainly one can argue the benefit of electing antiabortion candidates as a way eventually to have the issue considered. But given the overwhelming public preference for not re-criminalizing abortion, and given politicians' demonstrated preference to be led by their constituents, what argument supports the claim that elimination of abortion will result from voting for every antiabortion candidate? Here we need to recall that legislation and constitutional amendments are not the only way to stop abortions or to promote other aspects of a pro-life agenda.

Possibilities

There is another way to prioritize pro-life issues during an election campaign, a way that minimizes the dangers while offering possibilities for blending idealism and common sense practicality. This alternative approach may begin by asking which issues we consider top priorities. It then moves to a number of feasibility tests.

Foremost among these is the question of whether or not a particular issue has any chance of being addressed at this level of government. Let us suppose it is clear that the state legislature will not take up the issue of providing health insurance for children during the term of office for which these candidates are running. Is it morally responsible to vote for candidates according to where they stand on this or any issue that has no hope of being considered during this candidate's term of office? Would it not be more honest to consider a broader range of issues—including other pro-life issues—that are more likely to be addressed?

This kind of prioritizing considers what has a chance of finding its way into the legislative process. It does not diminish the importance of our personal views on an issue. Nonetheless, it does challenge us to appraise honestly what might be the most effective way of working on it. We may have to conclude that the legislative process is not where change is likely to happen, in which case it seems less than honest to measure candidates by where they stand on this issue.

There are many topics to consider when voting, many societal needs, and many ways to promote the common good. To enter into this requires that we not plant our feet into one or three or five cement buckets of "non-negotiable issues." That approach is not an honest exercise of civic responsibility. Neither is it an effective way of promoting a pro-life agenda today.

Following Our Passions

All of us can help promote a pro-life agenda through elections and the legislative process as well as through the many other ways already noted. How we do this may vary from one person to the next. We will not always agree on the issues to be addressed and the best means to address them. However, we should still be able to value these differences and recognize the fact that each of us may be drawn to different challenges.

Called to Different Causes

Not all of us will share the same passion for every topic or challenge facing our society. By our backgrounds and experiences we are drawn to different issues. We may know and accept the church's teaching on the death penalty or on abortion. That does not mean that these are the issues we feel most called to work on. Our work or profession or where we live can be factors that lead us to become involved with particular social needs.

No one should feel guilty because he or she is involved with one issue rather than another. We should honor and direct to good ends the passion we feel for a particular cause. Whether in volunteering or in voting every person should follow his or her heart in acting in ways considered most beneficial to the larger community. There is no moral mandate calling for all Catholics to agree on which issues must be addressed, on what political positions we must take, or on which candidates we should support. A well-formed conscience is our ultimate guide in these matters. That conscience is formed by the best possible understanding of these complex issues, by relevant church teachings, and by our own passion and inclination about current happenings within our society and the world.

Different Gifts

God has created each of us with particular gifts and talents. We use these gifts to meet our own needs as well as the needs of family members and others dependent upon us. But the gifts God has bestowed on us are intended also to help build up the larger community. This is what Catholic social teaching means by saying that each of us has a responsibility to contribute to the common good. There are many ways in which we do this. Voting is one way for all of us to participate in building healthy communities and a more just society. Beyond this overtly political act of choosing civic leaders, we contribute to the common good in many and varied ways.

How we choose to make our contributions will depend upon the energy we feel for different issues as well as the particular talents and gifts we have been given. Our moral responsibility is to nurture, develop, and then use these gifts to address whatever topic or issue is important to us. The challenge here is not that we have to agree on which issues to engage but that we work on whatever issue we feel drawn to. The passion God has given us for this issue and the talents given to work on it must not be ignored.

> *Our moral responsibility is to nurture, develop, and then use these gifts to address whatever topic or issue is important to us.*

For the Common Good

If each of us develops and uses what God has already given us, and if each of us becomes involved in issues that are important to us, then it is likely that together we will be working on all the important issues. Some of us may not have much energy or talent for working on early childhood development issues. Nonetheless, we can be grateful that other persons are involved in this important matter with passion and skill. We may have strong feelings about other topics like capital punishment. These are issues to which we must direct our energies and talents.

The point here is that not everyone is called to work on the same issues with the same level of commitment and skills. All of us need to recognize the seriousness of pro-life issues and where we might impact them. We need to see that all of these issues are related and that all of us have some connection to every pro-life issue. Beyond that we might recognize our respective roles as members of the church in promoting a pro-life agenda as part of the common good. This is material for the next chapter.

Discussion Points:

- To be pro-life means to resist any attacks against human life and to defend every person's right to whatever is needed to live that life in dignity.

- A pro-life agenda in politics, especially in voting, must not be restricted to any one single issue.

- Voting is not the only way—and sometimes not the most effective way—to address pro-life issues.

- A danger in prioritizing issues during an election campaign is that of focusing on only one or two issues.

- Each of us should contribute to the common good by following our passions and using the gifts received from God to work on the issues to which we feel drawn.

Chapter 6

Roles

The Catholic Church has not always been a friend of democracy.

Throughout the nineteenth century, church leaders expressed mistrust of ordinary people choosing governments, something about the untutored masses not being able to recognize what was best for them. But there can be no doubt that modern Catholic social teachings demonstrate a preference for democratic forms of governance. In that preference is a recognition that each citizen shares a responsibility to take part in such governance, at least at the level of electing leaders. This chapter focuses upon the obligation we all have to participate in political elections. It addresses the different roles that clergy and laity have in this process, as well as the challenges facing Catholics in following their consciences when they enter the voting booths.

Responsibility of All

Few would disagree that one duty of a good citizen is to vote in elections, a minimal expectation of persons enjoying the benefits of living in a democracy. To the extent possible, citizens also should take part in the election campaign process. Advocating or campaigning for particular candidates might be attractive to some, while others follow a less partisan path. This may include helping with voter education or voter registration efforts, or serving as an election judge during the voting.

Our most important contribution to a healthy electoral process, however, is to vote and to do so in an informed and conscientious manner. This necessarily suggests that in deciding how to vote we consider factors and issues beyond our personal wants. Catholic social teaching invites us to consider three major factors during an election campaign: 1) What are the larger community needs? 2) How might we best protect human life and dignity? and 3) How might we promote the interests of the poor and the marginalized?

Vote Community Needs

The first responsibility in deciding how to vote is to consider the needs of the larger community, what Catholic teaching refers to as the common good. What does our society require to promote those social and economic conditions that will allow everyone to do well? This is a broad question, inviting discussion of all issues and all needs faced by the community, state, or nation. Among these may be such topics as education and school funding, controlling costs of health care, identifying what is needed to foster healthier families, and providing for our nation's legitimate defense.

The decision on how to vote in a particular election should consider which candidate is most able and willing to address these community needs through the office to which she or he is elected. This requires that issues of concern to the larger community are in fact part of the election campaign discussions and debates. Voters, therefore, must insist that candidates address these topics. A good place for that to happen is in nonpartisan voter education forums designed to help the public learn candidates' positions on various issues.

Vote for Human Life and Dignity

A second set of issues that Catholic social teaching leads us to consider during election campaigns is that of protecting human life and dignity. One could easily argue that resisting attacks against human life is integral to promoting the common good. Defending the life of every human person and advocating for all human rights is essential to improving living conditions for everyone. These conditions include the possibility of living one's life until natural death as well as assurance of having food, housing, health care, and whatever else is needed to live that life in dignity.

From a Catholic perspective, these are important factors to consider when deciding how to vote. If we as a society are not able to defend human life and promote the dignity of all persons by ensuring human rights, there remains little of worth that we are able to accomplish. The political candidates for whom we choose to vote should have a demonstrated commitment to the common good that includes a willingness to defend life and foster the dignity of every human being.

Vote to Empower the Marginalized

A third priority to guide us in voting is the call to give particular attention to the needs of the poor and the marginalized. In Catholic teaching this is the preferential option for the poor. When faced with various options regarding public policies, laws, or programs, we are called to support those options that are of greatest benefit to persons who are the most marginalized in our society and throughout the world. This also means we vote for those candidates who share this commitment.

As already noted, this preferential option for the poor is rooted in biblical admonitions about caring for the widows, orphans, and strangers. It emerges from early Christian writings that the goods of the earth are intended to meet the needs of everyone. It is articulated in modern Catholic teachings which warn that the justice of a society is measured by how it cares for those who are most weak and most vulnerable. In weighing all this during election campaigns, an element of common sense should remind us that we as a society do well when everyone in this society does well, including those living on the fringes.

Church Leaders

During the months leading up to the 2004 presidential election a small number of Catholic bishops declared that candidate John Kerry, a Catholic, was not welcome to receive the Eucharist in their dioceses because of his position on abortion. With their statements airing on national television, these bishops caused a good bit of confusion among many Catholics. Were they speaking for the U.S. Catholic bishops as a body? Did their statements mean that Catholics could not vote for this candidate? At the very least this experience raised questions about the role of church leaders—particularly the ordained—during an election campaign.

Like any other citizen, priests and bishops have the right and duty to vote and to do so intelligently and with consideration of all the issues. Beyond that there are clear legal guidelines on what a priest or bishop, acting in the name of a parish or diocese, may do during an election campaign. The 501(c) 3 provisions of the United States' tax code prohibit churches from engaging in partisan political activity—that is, activity promoting a particular candidate.

Teachers

In spite of those limitations, church leaders have much to offer Catholics trying to decide how to vote. One of the primary responsibilities of bishops is to teach. Theirs is the official teaching of the Catholic Church and theirs is the responsibility to present the church's teachings on faith and morals. These teachings, especially regarding morals, are not left in abstract formulas and unintelligible theological decrees. Rather, the bishops often teach moral principles by relating them to issues of the day. Examples of this can be seen in such pastoral letters as For I Was Hungry (2005) or Global Climate Change (2001). In these statements the bishops remind us of Catholic moral principles related to food production and to caring for the environment.

As teachers the bishops often lift up issues that deserve attention from the Catholic faithful. This may happen at any time and sometimes takes the form of a teaching statement by the bishops of one state or even by a single bishop for his diocese. Since 1976 the United States Catholic bishops as a body have issued a pastoral statement on voting to coincide with the presidential elections. These statements present again the major themes of Catholic social teachings, and they remind Catholics of their responsibility to vote. Included in these statements every four years is a discussion of the many issues Catholics should consider as they make their decisions about how to vote. These statements from the bishops never tell Catholics how to vote, but they do urge us to consider the full range of issues and let our faith guide our voting decisions.

Prophets

Beyond teaching, the office of bishop carries a prophetic role. One of the ways bishops exercise their prophetic ministry is to point out something that is wrong in society, especially when the dignity of persons is threatened by the denial of human rights. For a very long time bishops have spoken out against abortion and in more recent decades against capital punishment. Today bishops as a body and in their dioceses are standing for the rights of immigrants. Often these prophetic statements are controversial and clash with popular sentiment. Frequently they point to social wrongs for which there may not be easy corrections.

In their prophetic role the leaders of the church need not have a solution to offer. Their primary task is to recognize a wrong, to name it, and to challenge members of the church as well as the larger society to address the issue. In this challenge rests a call to all of us to engage the issue and to examine our values and how we might be connected to the issue. Again, whether speaking or writing as teachers or prophets, the bishops do not tell Catholic laity how to vote. What they have to say, however, should become material for us to consider as we explore the candidates and the many issues that constitute an election campaign (Forming Consciences for Faithful Citizenship, 7).

Laity

The role of the laity during an election campaign is quite clear. It is our task to make the best possible choices on who should hold public office and lead us in building the common good. To do that responsibly and well we need to know what values are most important to us, we need to know the issues, and we need to know the candidates.

Know Our Values

Our core values are shaped by many factors and come from different sources—family, friends, school, culture, faith. One of our greatest challenges is to be intentional and reflective about our values. If we are not, the risk is great that we will uncritically accept values and norms that the larger society presents as standard for living the good life. These are not necessarily bad, but it often happens that our faith calls us to values different from those of our culture.

A good place to become familiar with faith-inspired values related to issues of our day is Catholic social teachings. These teachings offer moral principles and practical guidance for thinking about the social, economic, and political topics of our day. From these teachings the bishops draw norms by which to critique topics presented in timely pastoral letters. Catholic social teachings represent some of the most helpful, though challenging, sources for developing our values around today's issues.

Know the Issues

Our second challenge as we prepare to vote is to know the issues. This means being informed about current events and societal and global needs, what's happening around us and around the world. Each of us may choose a different source for the needed information that keeps us informed of the issues—radio, TV, internet, or other print publications.

A challenge here is to have at least relatively unbiased sources of news. In this day of extreme position talk shows and evening news programs that are quite light on news, this is not a small challenge. Responsible voting also requires that we be as informed about as many issues as possible and avoid the temptation to examine only one or two issues in which we have a strong interest. We may be working on certain community needs, but in preparation for voting we need to consider a broader range of issues.

Know the Candidates

Our third challenge is to know the candidates. While we should seek to know as much as we can about the candidates, our particular focus should be on where each candidate stands on a good range of issues. As the bishops reminded us in their 2003 statement, Faithful Citizenship, we the voters should "examine the position of candidates on the full range of issues, as well as on their personal integrity, philosophy, and performance" (p. 11).

The persons we elect to public office will take the lead in carrying out the functions of government. While all of us have a place in building up the common good, those in government have a special role in this. Theirs is the task of ensuring the minimum conditions that make it possible for everyone to live reasonably well. As voting citizens we share in this responsibility by helping to shape public opinion and by choosing our representatives.

Living with Disagreement

As we make our decisions about voting, it is inevitable that we will encounter disagreement among other citizens on which issues are the most important to consider in a particular election. Likewise, we may differ in our assessment of the candidates. That is the nature of a democracy and the consequence of a society that is marked by religious pluralism. We don't all work out of the same moral framework. Different faiths and different denominations within Christianity may emphasize different moral implications flowing out of their religious beliefs.

Even among Catholics there always will be a legitimate variety of options for promoting the common good, for advocating justice and human rights, and for creating the social and economic conditions that allow everyone to develop themselves fully. The church has long taught that the same Christian faith can lead to different prudential judgments regarding concrete issues. When Catholics find themselves in disagreement, two cautions from the social teachings bear repeating. One is that we try to understand one another's positions and presume good motives and intentions among those with whom we disagree. Second, when we differ over challenging issues facing society, we must not claim the church's authority exclusively for our personal positions.

Following One's Conscience

In the end each of us must vote as we are guided by our conscience. In this imperfect world where all of us bear the marks of human sinfulness, we never will find a perfect candidate. At whatever level of government we may be voting, no candidate will score 100 percent accuracy on every issue of importance to us. Nor will any one candidate measure up perfectly to the church's moral teachings on critical issues of our day.

> *Second, when we differ over challenging issues facing society, we must not claim the church's authority exclusively for our personal positions.*

In the absence of perfect candidates, it is all the more important for Catholics to vote on the basis of well-formed consciences. The foundation for such a conscience is knowing one's values, knowing the issues, and knowing the candidates. From a Catholic perspective the moral framework out of which to engage political issues and against which to evaluate candidates is a consistent ethic of life. This ethic includes the many issues already recognized as part of the pro-life agenda today. Even as we acknowledge the importance of all these issues, there still remains the task of deciding which of them are most important at this time and for the particular office for which the candidates are running.

Staying Focused

Making choices about issues and candidates is not an easy task. It can be made easier by a year-round effort at being informed. Following the news on a daily basis can help us identify the more pressing issues when election campaigns begin. That also can help us be less swayed by a few voices that would have us believe there are only one or two or five issues worthy of consideration. How to vote is a decision for each of us to make. To that end we would do well to try not to be swayed by a few loud voices claiming that Catholics must vote for certain candidates or that we must make our voting decision on the basis of a limited number of specified issues.

It is unfortunate that a few bishops should attract so much media attention by injecting the issue of communion reception into a political campaign. It is unfortunate that anyone would allow the Eucharist to become a political issue. When this happened in 2004, the result was confusion among many Catholics. By their statements these few bishops seemed to be suggesting that Catholics may not vote for any candidate who supports abortion. If we may not vote for a person who disagrees with the church's official teaching on abortion, presumably we may not vote for anyone who disagrees with the church's stand against capital punishment. Throw in a few more issues and it soon would be the case that Catholics simply cannot vote. There is no perfect candidate!

In deciding how to vote we need to stay focused on the issues and the candidates and let our values guide us in that decision. One of the most important sources to guide us in this is the United States Conference of Catholic Bishops. The bishops have given us numerous pastoral statements on how we should approach our responsibility of voting. Consistently they tell us to look at all the issues and take a broad view of how we might best promote the common good. Consistently they urge us to see that protecting human life means more than fighting for that life to be born. They tell us that promoting family life is about marriage and children, but it is also about education and just wages and accessible health care and affordable housing. They also tell us that working for the common good involves food security and caring for creation as well as providing justice for immigrants. When in the midst of an election campaign CNN reports that a bishop says Catholics should not vote for certain candidates or that we should focus on one or a few particular issues, that is the time to ask: what does the body of bishops say?

> *The teaching and prophetic voice of the bishops guides us in recognizing faith-based values related to issues and candidates. It is not the role of bishops to tell Catholics for whom they may or may not vote.*

Discussion Points:

- Catholic teaching suggests we consider three major questions as we decide how to vote: What are the larger community needs? How might we best protect human life and dignity? How might we promote the interests of the poor and the marginalized?

- The teaching and prophetic voice of the bishops guides us in recognizing faith-based values related to issues and candidates. It is not the role of bishops to tell Catholics for whom they may or may not vote.

- Responsible voting requires that we know our values, the issues of the day, and the candidates.

Chapter 7

Beyond Elections

"I thought election day would never get here!"

The day after elections can feel like the end of a long, difficult journey. For months politics have dominated the news and campaign ads have saturated radio and TV programming. Now all of that can fade away and our lives can return to normal. That is a common sentiment and understandable—as long as "normal" doesn't mean completely disengaging from politics until the next election.

Voting is one step in carrying out our civic and political responsibilities. It is not the first step and it should not be the last. Responsible voting is the fruit of a lifelong commitment to stay informed and to respond to needs in our local community and the larger society. That requires we stay engaged in the political and civic life of our communities both before and after elections. Beyond elections lie countless opportunities to help build a world that is more caring, more compassionate, and more just. The more we use these opportunities, the less likely we are to see elections as the one hope we have of addressing issues important to us. This chapter

discusses the importance of engaging in governance all
year round and every year. It also explores the religious
and moral perspectives we bring to public policy formation and the resources we have to guide us.

Engaging in Governance Year-round

Governance takes place at many levels. The big news
tends to develop around national or global issues—the
war in Iraq or the latest report on global warming or a
bridge collapse in Minneapolis that captures national
attention. These events in turn direct our attention to
national-level governing agents, such as the United
States Congress or the White House. It is difficult for us
to connect with these big news items, and so we trust
our elected officials to respond appropriately. That, we
believe, is how a representative democracy works.

While this kind of thinking is not wrong, it is also not
complete. It can lead us to disengage from the big happenings around the world that are dramatically and
sometimes tragically affecting other members of the
human community. It is this attitude that allows most
Americans to continue living their lives unaffected by
the fact that our nation is at war in Iraq and Afghanistan.
It is this attitude that makes it difficult to practice the
virtue of global solidarity as called for so often by the
late Pope John Paul II.

At All Levels

Handing over the big issues to our national leaders
is incomplete also because it inclines us to back away
from political responsibilities. Citizenship means being
engaged at different levels of governance—neighbor-

hood, township, city, county, state, and nation. Public leadership in each of these areas is critical to building healthy communities, to bringing about needed changes in society, and to fostering the common good.

None of us can be directly engaged in all of these areas because the daily demands of work, relationships, and family life fill most of our waking hours. But some of us might direct the talents and interests God has given us to one of these areas of governance. Becoming involved in political leadership is an important way to serve our neighbors and fellow citizens; it is a way to live out the biblical command to love our neighbor. That command, as seen in the teaching and actions of Jesus, carries the practical implications of addressing needs in front of us—like feeding the hungry, healing the sick, sheltering those without a home, visiting the imprisoned. Politics is the area in which major decisions on behalf of the common good are made. Each of us should consider whether direct political involvement might be the way we are called to help build a more just society and world.

At a minimum we must be attentive to what's happening in our communities, our society, and throughout the world. This is a necessary condition for voting responsibly.

Staying Informed

Granted, the majority of us are not likely to enter politics directly, yet we still have political responsibilities. At a minimum we must be attentive to what's happening in our communities, our society, and throughout the world. This is a necessary condition for voting responsibly. Staying informed of news and issues, however, is also a critical way for us to help build community beyond elections. This awareness empowers us to recognize whether elected officials are addressing issues discussed during the election campaign. It puts us in a position to encourage representatives to take on certain issues or to follow through on campaign promises.

Most important, keeping up with the news helps us to recognize the many opportunities we have to address certain topics. Public hearings, contacting legislators and other public officials, letters and columns in newspapers, entering into web discussions—all of these can be ways for us to have an impact on important issues of our day. To have such an impact, we must be informed. To participate knowledgeably in policy formation is a good way to experience that elections are not the only opportunity we have to address issues that are important to us.

Bringing a Religious Perspective

As people of faith, we have important contributions to bring to public policy discussions regarding economic and social issues. Our involvement in this task is itself a moral witness; we bring a religious vision of life and we offer guidelines to help sort out priorities and directions in policy formation.

A Moral Witness

Our first contribution is the witness that working to create a more just and caring world is a religious concern. It does matter how the economy is structured and whether working people are able to earn a wage that permits them to live a dignified life. It does matter that human behavior is causing global climate change that may bring unpredictable and catastrophic consequences. It does matter that more than thirty million Americans live in poverty and millions more are without health insurance. And all of this matters in a profoundly religious and moral sense.

Our participation in public discussions around contemporary news items is an expression of our belief that these issues cannot be defined solely in economic, national security, or cultural terms. These challenges facing our community or nation have moral dimensions as well. It is incumbent upon us as people of faith to let our faith guide us in assessing issues, in deciding on positions, and in articulating the moral questions. The prophets in the Old Testament and Jesus in the New Testament provide abundant examples of religious faith challenging "the way things are" in social, economic, and political matters.

A Religious Vision of Life

As Catholics we enjoy the benefit of a well-developed body of teachings related to the big topics of the day. Catholic social teachings provide the principles, norms, and moral framework for identifying ethical questions on important topics. It is not necessary that we all agree—even within the Catholic community—on how to answer these questions. But it is important that the questions are on the table.

These moral questions and the teachings from which they arise are all part of a faith-inspired vision of life in society. The objections we raise against the death penalty or embryonic stem cell research, or the concerns we voice about immigration or poverty rise out of this religious vision of the moral life and how society should be structured to promote that life.

The elements of this faith-based religious vision are present in the seven core themes of Catholic social teaching: dignity of the human person; call to family, community, and participation; rights and responsibilities; dignity of work and the rights of workers; preferential option for the poor; solidarity; and caring for creation. These moral teachings are a starting point for understanding how we are to live together as a society and as a human community. They are the practical norms for living our religious vision of life.

> *The elements of this faith-based religious vision are present in the seven core themes of Catholic social teaching: dignity of the human person; call to family, community, and participation; rights and responsibilities; dignity of work and the rights of workers; preferential option for the poor; solidarity; and caring for creation.*

Guidelines for Action

Engaging in year-round governance and in ongoing public discussions about contemporary issues is one way for each of us to contribute to the common good. It also is a way for us to teach others how to make their own contributions. Others might not agree with my position on euthanasia or raising the minimum wage, but my involvement in the debate can be a witness to the importance of having all views heard and discussed. Our faith calls us to be part of the discussions on this and other issues that impact the realization of human dignity. Though we may differ—even among Catholics—on the application of these teachings to specific issues, our first responsibility is to be part of the dialogue.

As Catholics we are bearers of a tradition that offers guidelines on how we should approach difficult topics. The first is to let the good of the larger community measure the value of any position we might take. How, for example, will society's ability to maintain and develop appropriate transportation infrastructure be affected by lowering or raising taxes? The Catholic emphasis upon the common good cautions us against taking positions that are shaped by excessive concern for my own benefit, especially if such measures might detract from the larger community.

A second guideline for our engagement in public discussions is to respect the life and dignity of every human person. We usually recognize that this means standing against abortion, euthanasia, assisted suicide, and capital punishment. We are not always as willing to recognize that this pro-life stance in Catholic moral teaching also means advocating for whatever is needed to allow people to live their entire lives in dignity—from conception to natural death. This touches such areas as food, housing, education, and health care.

A third guideline for sorting out ethical questions around debated issues is the Catholic emphasis on the preferential option for the poor. To promote the common good necessarily requires giving particular attention to the poor and the vulnerable. No one group can be excluded from our efforts to foster a healthy society. Every person and every group must be included in our considerations of how best to organize society. Our religious tradition reminds us as well that the measure of a just society is the degree to which it addresses the needs of its weakest members.

Policy Formation

Engaging in governance throughout the year is a way to be part of the process of reforming our own lives and restructuring society. We do this by daily efforts to keep ourselves informed of current issues, problems, and proposed solutions. When governing bodies take up an issue, we then are in a position to help decide what programs, regulations, and laws might best address the need at hand. This kind of policy formation is at the heart of the political process. It occurs every year, throughout the year, and it allows us to be involved in improving our society well beyond elections.

A Place for Institutional Change

Policy formation is one of the ways in which necessary institutional change occurs. In Catholic thought social or institutional change is closely connected to social justice. The latter means that each individual must contribute to the common good and that society must make that possible. Thus, if people are homeless or without health insurance or cannot earn a wage sufficient to provide for their family's needs, it is difficult for them to care for themselves, much less to focus on the needs of the larger community. That is why society must make necessary policy changes—perhaps to make more affordable housing available or to design some form of universal health insurance or to raise the minimum wage. Only then can we expect persons struggling in these areas to participate more fully in the life of the larger community. These changes (institutional, systemic, structural) are the goal of social justice and often come about through legislative policy changes. They represent a way to improve elements of society so that conditions exist that allow all to do well in order to build the common good.

Personal Transformation

Taking part in policy formation can help bring about needed social change. It can lead to personal transformation as well. To decide where we stand on a piece of proposed legislation is like deciding how we will vote in an election. Once again we are challenged to examine why we take the position we do, what leads us in one direction rather than another, and what values guide us. From a Catholic perspective one could argue that many policy issues should be evaluated by the three basic norms of promoting the common good, protecting the life and dignity of all persons, and giving special consideration to the poor and the marginalized. Though these norms may not apply to every policy issue, even a casual reading of daily newspapers reveals many issues under debate that directly relate to these norms. Whatever the topic, we must seek clarity on where we stand and why. We also must be prepared to change our hearts and let our resultant actions witness to the faith we profess to share.

Education and Advocacy

There can be little reason to claim ignorance on any important issue today. We have ready access to special TV news programming as well as an increasing number of web sites that offer comprehensive news along with respectable commentary. Various advocacy groups offer analyses of legislative efforts related to topics of interest to them. Likewise, the Catholic news media includes sources such as Catholic News Service, the *National Catholic Reporter,* and diocesan publications. All of these provide coverage of issues and analysis from the perspective of Catholic social teachings.

The critical point here is that it is not difficult for us to know what the issues are, how they are being considered by policy makers, and what values or moral questions we could bring to our engagement of these topics. If we are able to achieve such a level of awareness, then we have a moral duty to act. One action could be to advocate for legislative measures we judge important for the well-being of our society or our local community. There are many organizations and programs addressing issues of interest to us. We have no need to work alone, and we may strengthen such organized efforts by contributing our informed perspectives.

> *They speak of every person's obligation to pay taxes, but they never tell us how much we should pay.*

Resource Programs and Agencies

There are many resources to guide us in our involvement in governance throughout the year. Catholic social teachings are a starting point for evaluating, reforming, and shaping public policy to promote the common good.

These teachings do not tell us where we should stand on every issue. While they declare that every person has a right to needed medical services, the teachings do not tell us exactly how society should provide access to health care. They speak of every person's obligation to pay taxes, but they never tell us how much we should pay. The application of these moral principles to the concrete issues of our time is up to us. It is for us to determine what these norms suggest in terms of guaranteeing everyone's right to health care or regarding what is a fair and just tax burden. This is where we engage in public discussions around the issues, and this is where we allow our input to be shaped by moral considerations.

Still, the same teaching can lead many of us to take different positions. One source of guidance in this is to turn to the many faith-based organizations that address different social issues—Catholic, ecumenical, or interfaith. Many of these organizations provide the values-based analysis of issues that most of us don't have time to do. Looking at issues from an ecumenical or interfaith approach can help us appreciate why the non-Catholic majority of citizens in our country may not agree with Catholic teaching on one or another issue. Since politics and public policy formation require healthy compromise, it can be helpful to know where the give and take may need to occur.

Within the Catholic community we have helpful sources of guidance on public policy formation. Many parishes have social ministry (social concerns, social justice) committees to help parishioners know the Catholic social teachings and what these teachings have to say about particular issues. Such committees can help the entire parish through all its ministries to live out and give expression to the social mission of the church.

Most dioceses have a similar office whose purpose is to assist parishes in their social ministry. A particular service of the diocesan social concerns (social justice, social ministry) office is to provide education and training to parish leaders in this area of ministry. Related to public policy formation, these diocesan offices can be a link between parish social ministry committees and national or international programs of justice. This can be a particularly useful source of information related to current issues and the moral perspectives by which we might assess these issues.

On the state level, the local bishops often come together as the State Catholic Conference, the public policy arm of the bishops within the state. The primary task of these conferences is to advocate for public policies in the state legislature that promote the common good in accordance with Catholic social teachings. Obviously, the State Catholic Conferences are a good resource for Catholic parishioners to learn about current issues and their moral dimensions.

The United States Conference of Catholic Bishops (USCCB) contains many offices and programs working on legislative and public policy concerns at the national level. The USCCB represents the Catholic Church in all legislative and public policy matters at the nation's capital. Through this structure the Catholic bishops of the United States issue occasional pastoral letters in response to developments in the social, economic, and political areas. The USCCB also houses various programs addressing social justice issues. Among these we find the Catholic Campaign for Human Development, the Office of Migration and Refugee Services, and the Environmental Justice Program.

Discussion Points:

- A mark of good citizenship—and an excellent way to prepare for elections—is to remain engaged in public policy formation throughout the year.

- Working to create a more just and caring world is a fundamentally religious concern.

- Working for social change through public policy formation can lead as well to deep personal transformation.

- As Catholics we have abundant resources within the church to support our efforts to help build a more just society and world.

Conclusion

Political involvement, according to some Christians, does not find a strong foundation in the Scriptures, especially the New Testament. Jesus did not actively participate in the political sphere, so why should Christians? A quick response is to note that the society in which Jesus lived was not exactly a democracy. His opportunities for political engagement were few.

A more thoughtful response to this question might point out that Jesus called his followers to love one another and to show that love through practical acts of mercy and charity—feeding the hungry, sheltering the homeless, visiting the sick, and giving drink to the thirsty. But to love as Jesus commanded means more than responding to our neighbor's immediate needs. It means also striving to change whatever causes that neighbor to depend upon our charity—it means working for justice in our society and in the world. One way to do this is by choosing leaders who are committed to such change.

We do not live in the first-century Roman Empire. In this democratic republic that we call the United States of America, we the citizens choose the leaders who will guide our society. We determine whether or not our nation will be led by officials committed to building a society where every person is able to live a dignified life. Our faith leads us to this task and guides us as we engage the political areas of our lives. Our faith—our religion—calls us to political involvement.

Catholic theology reminds us of three public concerns that should inform our voting decisions. One is that we choose leaders committed to the common good, leaders who will ask what our society needs in order for everyone to do well. A second is that we vote for candidates who recognize that in order to promote the common good we must give particular attention to the needs of those who are less well off—the widows, orphans, and strangers of our time. A third is that we support candidates who are willing to protect human life and dignity. This means resisting all direct attacks against human life, and it means working to make sure all persons have what is necessary to live free of excessive dependence and want.

When we go to the polls, all of us should support a pro-life agenda. Equally important, we must recognize that being pro-life, and supporting a pro-life agenda, means more than simply being antiabortion. As we engage that agenda—in voting and in our ongoing political involvements—we should follow our passions and work on those issues that have a particular appeal to us. In that way we honor the special gifts, talents, and feelings God has placed in each of us.

Responsible voting means following our conscience, a conscience formed by knowing our values, the issues, and the candidates. We do not wait for others to tell us how to vote, but we do vote with the conviction that this is an action guided by our faith. From this civic involvement we gain so much, because voting and working year round to build a more just society and world is not only a religious concern but also an action that will lead to our personal conversion and renewal.